Salespreneurship:

Sales +

Entrepreneurship

How to Succeed as a Zero-Base Startup

Taesoon Shin

Copyright © 2018 Taesoon Shin

All rights reserved.

Prologue

Sales can be a terrifying task for some people. Some people might panic when they have to sell products to total strangers. This sales phobia cannot be easily addressed with mere skills or tips. The sales process should be accompanied by perceptions and actions that will lead to a shift in fundamental thinking towards sales. And it also takes a great deal of time and effort to get there. By all means, if you apply the method of this book's sales approach, it will lead to a dramatic reduction of time and effort.

I'm confident about the sales approach I'll discuss in this book, because I also had a big phobia about sales in the past, and I also panicked when I had to sell something in front of total strangers. But now, I have totally overcome the fear. After failing to pass the exam to become a government officer in Korea, I started sales when I was a senior in college. I studied sales and took many sales training courses, and some of them were very expensive courses.

In the process, someone like me who has a serious fear of sales needed a systematic approach to the unconscious level, so I also visited teachers from the relevant field to address my problems. I also felt the necessity of studying the *Book of Changes* (a Chinese classic on divination) and other Chinese texts to apply my understanding to sales. To learn how to build the trust, attitude and language proficiency, I visited the best entrepreneurs and CEOs of Korea. However, I felt all this was not enough. Therefore, I listened to lectures on marketing channels covered in Korea. Still, that wasn't enough either, so I registered on consulting services while paying about the annual salary of an employee of a small company to learn the famous marketing tools that became popular overseas.

I bought and tested all of the unfamiliar marketing tools from overseas and took courses from overseas marketers. After traversing the learning curve, I was able to produce remarkable sales results by finding and applying the applications that could be used in Korea.

With this knowledge, I've been able to develop Butterfly Investment in Korea, which for the fifth year is spreading the know-how on starting a business without capital. Now I call this business model the *zero-base startup*.

This was possible when I met Mr. Choi Gyu-Cheol, the chairman of the organization who planted the worldview of the non-capital startup business (zero-base startup) and launched new lectures and ideas each time.

Now I have an offline lecture— "Sales Is First!"— which was originally launched by Choi. He was also a long way from being a salesperson but turned into an amazing sales machine during his career. I tell the stories about his experiences in the lecture. From this lecture, more and more CEOs of startups have changed since I got to know them, and they are reborn as powerful sales promoters. With the launch of real sales skills, the entrepreneurs began to shine, and their voices began to feel relaxed and powerful. Gestures became natural, and above all, the love affair with their product began to grow. They were gradually turning into real businesspeople who wanted to solve customer problems with sincerity.

Those who could not even sell a single pencil are now able to lecture in public, sell high-priced goods, boost their self-esteem instantly, and create a steady stream of positive influence among the people around them. All this has led to an unconscious approach to sales fears while increasing confidence in how to start a business from scratch based on the results.

Now I began to advocate *salespreneurship*, a combination of "sales" and "entrepreneurship." Salespreneurship is the entrepreneurial spirit that puts sales first. If you want to start a business that is innovative, challenging and has a good impact, you have to start selling or sales. In the beginning stage of startups, entrepreneurs must be broken, bumped up, and then grow with sales before they can scale up their business safely and innovatively.

If I were naturally good at sales, I would never have coined the term salespreneurship. The intense fear of sales that I had in the past has rather blessed me. In the process of overcoming the fear by any means necessary, I have created the term salespreneurship. To set up salespreneurship, Butterfly Investment created a number of successful startup cases and coaching practices. I tried to include many examples of such cases in this book, making it more realistic, and to help my readers easily understand the process. In this process, the know-how and business model of the startup companies that we created are revealed without filtering.

Some readers will appreciate it while others will not.

While I was writing, I tried to be as honest as possible. It's true that it's difficult to inspire others unless we include examples and stories from our company and our own experience.

If you read with excitement the words "You're about to realize the details of what our companies have learned," then you'll be convinced 10 times stronger than if you only read them otherwise. And please read the words more than twice, that's because there's hidden know-how like jewelry that can only be seen at that time.

Unlike when working on my previous book, I was having a hard time writing this one. I kept asking myself if I had grown substantially before starting to write. Finally, after I was confident in answering proudly, I could start writing. Again, the script was completed after a long period of agony and growth after the project was launched.

I would like to express how grateful I am for having teachers who helped me grow significantly every time.

Thanks to the support of my lovely wife, Jihye; my son, Yoon Jae; my brother and his family; and parents from both sides of the family, I am happy every day. I always remember that I'm here thanks to my co-founders, who have started new businesses without any capital with Butterfly Investment, and nearly 1,000 members of Butterfly Investment. With this book, I'd like to reassure my belief once again to give more inspiration and to create synergies.

I'm also thankful for my real friends and colleagues who stayed beside me and supported me during the hard times.

I appreciate publishers who helped me make this book and publish it for the world.

Finally, I would like to express my heartfelt congratulations to the readers who will be able to completely break the old frame of the sale, and master salespreneurship to come across a surprisingly safe and enjoyable entrepreneur's way.

Although I wrote this book by myself, my first start was a lecture given by Choi, the co-founder of Butterfly

Investment. So I decided to publish this book because I was very fortunate to inherit his knowledge.

If you read this book over and over again, you'll be able to apply the following three things for your startup.

First, you can start a business and earn money from scratch. Butterfly Investment's initiative is based on pre-sales. How can you start a business when you don't have money? Everyone has to be suspicious. You can make the money you need through sales to grow your business. You can change the perception that you can't start a business without money. It's my job to enlighten my founders and teach them they should "sell first" and take it to heart that "sell first" principle comes first. We've gone all the way from reducing our resistance to sales to making our sales more fashionable, and managing sales follow-up. All this is covered in the book, and I provide some examples of selling the product first then starting a company.

Second, you'll be able to experience the things that might make your business go wrong. Zero-base startups make the least amount of products by raising funds from pre-sales and building the least number of services first. Based on that, they make more sales, set up a company with funds from pre-sales, and make homepages. We concentrate solely on making sales and only execute expenditures from the money we earn and do not even use credit cards to cover costs. This process is actually the same path people take just to go out of business and will have to start a business again.

If someone tries to start a zero-base business—a business without any capital—he or she can experience the situation of business failure and develop the know-how to overcome it. It's possible to feel how intolerable and lonely this process is and to develop an entrepreneurial spirit that breaks the ice as it overcomes difficulties. My idea of a real entrepreneurial spirit is not to rely on money and not to solve problems in a predictable way.

The business model new to the world.

The ability to execute a project fiercely.

The elicitation of brilliant ideas.

The sales skills with sophisticated attitudes and language.

These concepts direct this entrepreneurial spirit.

If you don't even know the size of your vessel, but want to stick to the amount of money you want to hold, you should first experience failure to prevent yourself from breaking the vessel you had. If you're good at borrowing money and receiving good investments, you might be much worse off. It's so hard to put back together the broken vessel at that time. To practice what went wrong from the beginning to not collapse later on is to start a business without any capital, and to start a business based on sales, not based on investments. Through this book, you'll find out how safely you can experience business failure.

Third, you'll be able to balance your life and career with your startup.

There's an expression *"work-life balance"*. You can balance your life even if you start a business. In fact, within the framework of life, business startups are included. I've stressed for a long time that I can speed up my personal growth and make it a process of performance through my business.

It isn't necessary to give up your life for your own business or to give up your own business for your own sake. The two are as compatible as it can be. And the balance should be adjusted by moving without stopping. When you realize that your scale isn't balanced, that it's constantly in and out of motion and that it's also balanced, you can lead a life through your own business.

A stationary balance is only possible when you die. If you stick to such a balance, you'll never find one that's conducive to life. When you find yourself in a state of active equilibrium, you can enjoy your startup.

The book also discusses the relationship between mental cultivating of CEO and business startups. It contains stories about balancing business and life, about incorporating mindfulness into making sales, and the mental training that will help you work proactively with customers and competitors.

I study and carry out my work every day in a way that nobody else in the country can do better, by connecting business startups and meditation. I'm confident that you can feel my confidence while you read the book.

About the Author

Saying that "creation is a fun, money-making game and the best tool to perform,"

Taesoon Shin is the founder of Butterfly Investment, contents creator, and also singer and dancer. He has discovered the link between start-ups and spirituality, and continues to spread this sprit through numerous writings and videos.

Moreover, Shin is doing coaching focusing on changes in unconsciousness allows entrepreneurs to find answers for themselves to have successful business.

Currently, Shin is running Butterfly Investment, focusing on Zero-base Startup business (Guiding businesss owners to start their business with no money, or no investment). Butterfly Investment in Korea, which for the fifth year is spreading the know-how on Zero-base Startup created a number of successful startup cases and coaching practices based on the Zero-base Startup.

His other books are "I work four hours a week and make 10 million won" and ""The Pirates' Startup Story" (only available in Korean):

If you are interested about the author and Butterfly Investment, please contact to below:

Email: Jihyekim.825@gmail.com

Instagram: www.instagram.com/shintaesoon

Web page: butterflyinvest.com

© 2018 Taesoon Shin. All rights reserved

Table of Contents

Prologue 3

About the Author 12

Chapter 1: The Key to Zero-Base Startups: Salespreneurship 18

   1. Who's going to buy something like this? Somebody will. 18

   2. A Lecture is sold without a single curriculum. .. 23

   3. Long-running businesspeople, long-running celebrities. 30

   4. If startups are doing business like big companies do, they will certainly fail. 35

   5. Six steps to expand customers as entrepreneurs of zero-base startups (startups with no capital). 40

   6. Why Butterfly Investment insists on pre-sales. .. 47

   7. Break the stereotypes of pre-sales first. 55

   8. Five points to make pre-sales successful. 60

   9. Why a six-digit income isn't so difficult for anyone to achieve. 67

10. Find a partner who really can do sales............. 74

11. Sell intangible products first for real sales. 80

12. The Fourth Industrial Revolution: Salespreneurship is a must-have............................ 87

13. It's a great illusion that the value increases only if it's added. 93

Chapter 2. Salespreneurship-Mind 101

1. The limit of the word "sales." 101

2. Why you can't take the lead in your sales........ 108

3. Without exception, sales always come first. 116

4. Ask forgiveness, not permission....................... 123

5. If you want to make the perfect product, start selling it when it isn't. 129

6. The power of pre-sales to strengthen the confidence of the founder. 135

7. Don't try to find something that looks good. Make what you do now successful. 141

8. Four typical types of customers the entrepreneur will encounter. 149

9. There is no meaningless work done in vain. 156

10. The limits of writing 100 times and how to overcome them. 162

11. The secret of imagination to dramatically increase sales capabilities. 167

12. Peace of mind vs. sales growth, a delicate correlation. 173

13. To the founders who wouldn't sell. 180

Chapter 3. Salespreneurship action. 187

1. we are selling 500-dollar pencils. 187

2. Sell proudly; create real value. 192

3. If you make it good and sell it cheap, you'll go bankrupt. 200

4. Three ways to build trust initially for pre-sales. 207

5. After all, sales are the first priority for all businesses. 213

6. The secret "4 Ps" to make your customer buy. .. 221

7. Sales know-how: Draw a picture inside the customer's mind. 229

8. It takes time for the customer's wallet to open. 234

9. Five things to keep in mind for startup companies not to fail. 239

10. Three things easily missed when presenting a sales seminar. 246

11. The 100 x 100 x 100 method to operate sales automation. 251

12. Data analysis and A/B tests and sales 257

Epilogue 264

About the Author 270

Chapter 1: The Key to Zero-Base Startups: Salespreneurship

1. Who's going to buy something like this? Somebody will.

While on Facebook, I watch the ads attentively. I read the lines used in advertisements, see how they're being edited in video clips, and get ideas from them. Advertising gives you a lot of interesting inspiration, and at the same time, you can see the types of products that are selling well and are trendy. One product I frequently saw on Facebook was a part of a cosmetics brand.

Most of the cosmetics are advertised on video. At the beginning of the commercial, a person with skin problems appears on the screen and the ad shows the changes that results from using the cosmetic product. The commercial shows the person using the products daily and the dramatic shift in this person's face a week or a month after using the cosmetics.

Besides cosmetics, diet products have also produced many video advertisements using a similar concept. They quickly show what someone looks like before they eat, how much they weigh, what they eat over a month, and what they eat currently. In the end, the video shows the user's changed appearance. I've even seen video clips of something similar for adult products. They also say in the video that they made $100,000 in sales just a few days after the ads were launched.

Diet, appearance, and health-related products are the most direct products that can touch consumers' instincts. And it seems that many people are trying to start a business in these fields because they have a good margin ratio (gross profit ratio). It's good to see better products developed and benefits them and to have confidence in their ability to produce results. However, it's hard to withstand fierce competition if one only considers the products to which one is instinctually drawn to be lucrative, and only start with the related products.

While looking around for more lucrative, provocative products that sell well in the market, it's easy to forget about the initial intention of starting a business. While it's meaningful to survive the rat race with best-selling products or products that are likely to sell well, it's more meaningful for the founder to make products that fascinate him or her.

If you've already started a business or have much experience in sales, you probably would agree. It's difficult to maintain a business with a sense of excitement if it's not one of your favorite products but makes a reasonable margin, or if the owner deals with products that don't suffer losses when they sell them, or if they can boost sales with just simple keywords or SEO ads. I have a natural desire to mount a new challenge, to do a business that isn't obvious, and I want to find an item only I can do. However, since people tend to find products that are just selling well in the market, they can't come up with other new ideas. In the classroom, I often tell them about the ridiculous products being sold.

Such is the case of the company that sells the land of the moon. Who would buy the land of the moon? But people, including celebrities and a former president of the United States, have bought this product. What's even more interesting is that the company sells the lands of Mars and Venus too. It's a company that sells not only the moon but also the universe. Isn't this fantastic just to imagine?

If you think what you're about to sell is ridiculous, and you're hesitant because you don't think the public will recognize it, then watch these examples and be brave. I'm sure someone will show up and buy your product. You only have to look for someone like you. Ninety-nine out of 100 will turn a blind eye to it, but one of them will praise the product you sell and become a fan.

I can't help but mention a company that sells trash produced in New York City. Justin Gignac, the founder of NYC Garbage, sold beautifully packed garbage on the streets of New York to test the importance of packaging. However, many people throughout the country flooded the company with orders for New York "perfume."

Transparent containers with a trash can cost from $50 to $100. (Note: Throughout this book, the dollar sign [$] sign and the word "dollars" indicate US dollars.)

Some packages aren't just trash, they also have a significant relationship to certain events. Of course, they're more expensive. For example, there's a limited edition of collected trash from the presidential inauguration of Barack Obama. These limited items are so popular that they sold out immediately. People are cheering for garbage.

How about this? I believe the new product you choose to sell must be better than trash. You can find someone like you. Though 99 out of 100 may turn you away, one of them will be excited by your product and want to buy it. Now that we've talked about selling trash, we're going to move on to the next level.

In 1961, an artist named Piero Manzoni put his poop in a can and sold it to the rich based on the value of gold, about $40 at that time. The can was even auctioned off in 2007 for 170 million won. The product you're going to sell cannot be less attractive than poop.

If the public doesn't see the attractiveness but feels your conviction and charm, then it can be appealing to people like you. Ninety-nine out of 100 people cannot see this. But one of them will be a big fan.

As soon as we limit what we sell, we sell what others sell. The example above is not immediately suggesting that extreme products be sold at random. I mentioned these examples to show how many restrictions we place on our startup items and products we plan to sell.

When choosing a startup item, the founder is afraid that it's the only item he's attached to. They fear that the public will not recognize it. Instead of selling products that many people are interested in, the startup owner who is more likely to sell products that are of interest to a small number of people has a higher chance of success in the long term.

That's because it's easy for a founder to build a brand that's unique, and is more likely to win through creativity than competition for startups. Of course, if you look for someone like yourself, you may find things go slowly at first. But as one or two people buy the products and are satisfied by them, they tell people what they purchased. As a result, there's a community, and the products become known to the world as original best-selling products.

Butterfly Investment has several cofounded companies, and most of the products from cofounded companies are growing this way. We don't deliberately choose items that are likely to sell well in the market. Instead, the founder makes his items with affection, and that offer a solution to his own problems in his life, and a solution to problems similar to his.

In this way, a company can last for a long time, and it creates a unique brand. Don't set limits to what you can sell unless you seriously invade morality. There's no law that requires selling only what the public wants. That would apply to the big companies. I wonder who will buy the products, but there are always more people to buy them than I thought. Unless you give up.

2. A Lecture is sold without a single curriculum.

It's hard to imagine that a lecture is being sold without a curriculum in hand. But if you go further and hear that the lecture is being sold without a lecturer, you'll think it doesn't make sense at all.

As I put in my previous books, the process of growing my business and the stories my teachers told while I was learning how to run the business were not related in any way. And there wasn't a thing that didn't really come out of the field. I take pride in that more than anything else. Inexperienced people would call it sophistry and a far-fetched idea, but I proudly wrote about those experiences. This was because my teachers actually experienced those uncommon things and achieved success from failures in real life.

I take pride in the ability to talk about the events that go beyond common sense, and I haven't had a greater pleasure than this. When I try to break down "common sense" again in this chapter, my heart beats faster. I've been giving lectures on different topics for about 25 weeks since I began writing a book. I have a big lecture titled "The Law of Startups Without Failure," But there's no such thing as a table of contents in the introduction of the lecture or a fixed curriculum prepared earlier.

Those interested in knowing about the business ecosystem that I created after meeting with Choi, (the co-founder of Butterfly Investment), and those who want to know about my previous books can come and take the class. There will be more questions to ask and greater communication with one another than in any other class for startups. Every week, I prepare a topic I would like to present in a mini-lecture format. The concept for the day is usually set a day before or on the lecture day.

I took the challenge of producing more than 10 pages of business-idea documents every week. These was successfully executed for 150 weeks without any delays or cancellations. For me, this kind of lecture, without pre-set curriculum, became another huge challenge, but it was more than a typical challenge. Already, Choi had been giving lectures on different topics for about a year. Preparing and presenting different lectures each week isn't easy, but getting used to doing so gives you the ability to focus and concentrate on living a week like a month.

As such, the fact that the lecture is being sold at a set price and the subject isn't decided in advance makes it seem absurd. But what's more surprising is the existence of a weekly seminar. Here, both the lecturer and the lecture topic aren't disclosed until people come to the class. This seminar has been held successfully for more than two years. The lecture is titled "A Lecture." It's organized by School Monster, and Choi is the leader of the school.

This weekly seminar— "A Lecture"—is promoted without any information. Literally, it's a lecture. You can't tell from the introduction of the lecture on the School Monster website which lecturer will be coming. According to the introduction of classes and instructors posted on the website and public relations site, it's proudly described as "nondisclosure." The person who would become a lecturer of "A Lecture" is thoroughly explored by School Monster.

Choi picks a teacher every week who can tell honest and resonant stories. The teacher is not a professional. Through this lecture, they have the special experience of making their debut as instructors. Of course, those who attended the lecture and thought it was below their expectations may request refunds. But this is rarely the case. Many of the lecturers sympathize with the philosophy of Butterfly Investment and agree on the idea of having no capital in advance to start the business. This makes them take note of lectures held by Butterfly

Investment. The lecturers agree on the spirit of starting a zero-base business, and because of such attributes, there's a lot to say as a lecturer.

They are confident in the fact that the way they lived in the past cannot guarantee happiness in the future. So they are told that they are pursuing their own paths during the difficult process, and are too ideal and unrealistic. People who want to pursue extraordinary lives and think differently about extraordinary things come to Butterfly Investment to find ways of starting a business without capital after overcoming many challenges.

They have one amazing story in their lives and set an inspiring example. Also, they have found a good way to change their lives. They are the ones with the conviction to pursue their own paths no matter what other people say and have pure hearts like children. Choi and I are confident in leading this path. The first time they put themselves on stage, they will work hard to create a turning point with this "A Lecture." So they work hard to prepare a PowerPoint presentation, and practice standing on the stage for "A Lecture." There are stories of raw stuff that are not to be heard in the lectures of famous teachers on professional PowerPoints and in polished language. Hence, it's appealing to hear stories that are closer to the lives of those who come for the lectures.

Will a lecture without an introduction or without an introduction of a lecturer sell? We all suspected it would, but it became a steady, best-selling lecture for over two years up till now. They're demonstrating their successful progress by applying the sales and the preparation to the opening of the lecture as well as to the business. But in fact, a different location is where this approach and pre-selling will be effective.

I'm training people who want to go to the extent of starting a zero-base startup. I'm developing CEOs who are well equipped with sales skills, helping them build a new business ecosystem without any investment or capital while also generating sales revenue. I've been teaching every week for about five years, but I never thought back then that I would do this.

However, Choi, the chair of the group, said, "We should continue teaching because we need to develop our sales skills offline, improve our ad-lib skills, and our communication skills." So I evolved. Standing in front of others, making impromptu comments, and coping with embarrassing situations were all abilities I definitely lacked. However, ironically, now these have all become my most confident abilities. It's not too much to say that I feel like I'm living a second life.

I felt I wasn't very good at lecturing. People who are good at making presentations in college seem to be gifted. However, I experienced it myself that it can be learned, and this opened the second act of my life. I've learned that if I start the lecture and run it weekly, I can't help but do it well. Someone such as Choi encouraged people to do so. And members of Butterfly Investment have encouraged one another. They should be able to deal with the public and convey exactly and truly what they intend to say both offline and online. This directly leads to sales. But if you put off giving lectures on the ground that you don't have any experience in lecturing about, and if you give up the lecture because you have stage fright, you'll actually end up failing to make progress through zero-base startup.

I'm not saying you can start a business if you give a good lecture right now. You can get used to things you didn't think you could do in the past. These experiences become confidence and help to engage the customer. Becoming a lecturer or speaker is a prerequisite for successful startups. So we urge people who are serious about starting a business without any capital to try giving any lecture in front of others. At the initial stage, nearly 90 percent of people are hesitant.

"I'm not ready for it yet." "I haven't made a strong proposal yet." "I should have made a more complete one." I can truly understand these concerns because that's the way I started my career. The beginning was similar to the startup of the new business, which is now carried on by lectures.

You won't find the reason that you shouldn't start anything until you start. Therefore, if we put off the beginning continuously, we should take extraordinary measures even if it feels contrary to our nature. When people want to choose a startup item and start a business actively, they put up a lecture introduction and an introduction of teachers to the website, even if they don't have a lecture plan yet. So they must lead the class as announced on the website initially.

In this way, countless instructors and business salespeople are produced. The system shocked the people who kept procrastinating and helped them start a new life. If a lecturer is making an attractive class and people begin attending, the lecturer cannot help but make the class much better. Most of the people who put off the lecture started this way, and they're improving constantly as they develop the lecture every week. Making pre-sales has a powerful effect on stopping procrastination. If you think you want to become a lecturer, but if you put it off continuously, you can choose to sell it first or announce it to the public first.

Announce the introduction and topic of the lecture that will likely be sold later. And when people register for the lecture, then you should make a lecture according to the introduction. Be sure to remember that the majority of people sell and announce first, and then they prepare a lecture. If you make the lecture perfect first and try to sell it, you may delay giving it forever. Sell it first, and prepare the lecture later.

3. Long-running businesspeople, long-running celebrities.

"I don't know when the money is going to be coming in, and if I just do my job diligently, will everything be okay?"

In fact, money can come to someone quickly, or it can come late. But I think how much you enjoyed your work before that time is more important than worrying about the money. That's because the past can never be bought with money. If you waste your time complaining about having no money and keep on dragging yourself to work, you can't enjoy the money even if it comes in later.

It doesn't mean much to keep plugging away at other people's favorite things or just to find a lucrative job even if you don't like the product or work. There's always going to be someone more passionate about the product and business. And since they came to the business not because they liked it, but because they wanted to make money quickly, impatience follows them everywhere. They're bent on finding a shortcut, but this only leads to bad luck or waste. Then they start snooping around other areas.

We have seen many cases in which after more than a decade of getting bit parts and acting in roles portraying minor characters, someone became a big star after being recognized as a new style setter in TV dramas and movies. It's not easy to make money in a play. The actor earns a part-time income while trying to support themselves and, perhaps, a family. They want to act on the stage so much that usually, they must also work a second job such as manual labor or waiting tables. Then, with such devotion, the actor who puts his energies into the play has a chance at last.

The same is true for singers who have gone through a long period of being unknown. Even if they don't have much money, they're gradually recognized when they sing in front of a small number of fans. They keep doing this and keep making songs and perform in front of others which then finally gain popularity in the major market. Then their popularity persists. Even if their popularity declines, they've had a long history of not being famous, so they're ready to play their role while staying true to their art. Fast-crafted singers, such as those who have undergone a relatively short period of training and are produced after generous support from their respective companies, may come out and gain popularity fast, but they can't count on a long-running career.

If you're preparing to start a business, or if your goal is to be free from your full-time job in the future, you'll need to conduct a variety of studies but you should especially analyze celebrities. I consider celebrities a kind of businesspeople, and they have lots of common characteristics. They promote their talents and content, so they make money. They also use different strategies to raise their value per hour. Sometimes, they don't participate in live shows or comedy programs on purpose or appear in certain commercials. They select when to appear in photos for the public and when not to be seen. These are all image-management strategies.

When they aren't popular and have no money, they should work without a management company or an agency. Even without a manager, they should style their hair and makeup, do their own driving, and check their schedule. As they do so, they slowly become known to people and even to a handful of fans. Then, they take care of their loyal fans. These events are constantly building on one another, making the person better known, making them work harder, and making good work in front of the producers and directors. Using this as a stepping-stone, they can also do promotional blasts and increase their fan base. With a hike in the price of their appearances in big commercials, they gradually move to the next level.

If it's not easy to meet successful people after starting a business, it's good to study some of the top celebrities you're interested in. Some of the top stars may become famous overnight, while others may be stars after a long period of obscurity. Some celebrities have a bad image at first, but eventually develop a good one, while others have a good image at first and develop a bad one later on.

What kind of celebrity or entertainer would you like to become as a businessperson? There are some stars who have built their skills for a long time before their debut,

but there are others who become stars overnight because they are so lucky as to have good connections. They all look like stars to us. And we envy their splendor, wealth, and connections.

However, one day you get the news that one of those stars suddenly became corrupted or made an extreme choice, doing drugs or alcohol. Why does anyone who has that many fans and such good fortune make that choice? In fact, this happens even among those who are called successful startups.

Businesspeople often feel extremely lonely, unable to handle the success, money, and connections they're fortunate to get. Neither the second nor third generation of a very wealthy family are happy. Having a lot of money doesn't make them happy in their daily lives, and they often must handle the difficult news.

Long-running business people have something in common with long-running entertainers or actors. They're the ones who do what they want to do. Whether it's good or bad, whether they earn a large sum of money or not, people who have continued to work at their own pace are making it in the long run.

Songs from indie or older singers who constantly create their albums without sticking to their hit songs are coming out and becoming popular in the end, and things are happening a long time after the release. From small-sized production companies that aren't major players of Korean Pop, we see the example of Bangtan Boys (BTS), which have been called top artists by Billboard.

They performed musical activities that show their skills regardless of their rank and managed them well from their small fan base, and it was just the start of their fame. With social networking occurring daily and the rate of reliance on regular broadcasting and advertising declining, the star's survival strategy is changing. People who are constantly active for their audience and stick to their true colors without expecting a shortcut are eventually recognized. And they are loved for a long time, doing the activities they want to do without major ups and downs.

Well, what kind of celebrity business would you like to be? Do you want to be a big star one night but fades by the next night? Or do you want to be a shining star for a long time?

Unbreakable entrepreneurs, who don't seek a shortcut based on their money but scale up with sales experience from the bottom, choose to be small at first but long-lasting stars.

And I hope I'll meet readers on this road with happy faces for a long time. At the same time, before the immediate popularity and the big money, we should be humble. We can start with a handful of customer management skills, selling harder, making smaller but valuable money. So I wish to shine on the world for a long time together.

4. If startups are doing business like big companies do, they will certainly fail.

A certain educational institution sells gift certificates worth $20,000 for VIP programs. How do you feel when you hear these stories? "Oh, that's very expensive, is it true?" You might think this way. However, the composition of the product shows that it's a gift certificate that can be used for a couple of lectures worth $50,000 in total and can be used continuously until the company closes the business.

How do you feel about the 20-million-won price—$20,000—after hearing this story? The price is a bit high but understandable. There are so many online services overseas selling this way. There are a great number of captivating services, such as automatic mailing programs and automatic posting programs on Facebook.

These services cost $100 on a monthly basis, but if you pay once a year, they're discounted up to only $500, making a big sale at one time. It's cheaper to pay $100 right now, but some customers would benefit from paying $500 at one time if they used the service for the long run.

In these instances, you'll feel that high prices can be reasonable. Butterfly Investment has a reason to offer a one-year, three-year, or more of its services as a product. It provides long-term services so that it can sell them as high-priced. It doesn't mean to overcharge for no reason. Even though they pay large amounts of money at one time, people are naturally satisfied when they think they need long-term training and constant feedback, if the company provides proper service accordingly.

We can make any kind of expensive model so that both the client and the company can win. However, if you, as a startup company, try to provide services to multiple customers like a large company does, it's difficult to survive. When you manage a small number of customers and provide the right service with sufficient funds, you'll also be able to increase customer satisfaction and achieve the goals you want.

If you're running a startup that has a low-priced product and a large number of customers, but a low level of customer satisfaction, high volume of fixed costs, and no immediate follow-up with customers, you must stop and renovate your business model immediately. In the long run, it's a situation in which business models are being managed without any future vision.

Once again, I would like to emphasize the importance of *not* benchmarking the way conglomerates or large companies operate. There is a different business model for startups.

If you're just starting up a small company, you shouldn't make the mistake of benchmarking a large company. Big business already has a solid infrastructure and a large capital pool, and it's based on a large pool of people. Accordingly, it's possible to create and manage 100,000, one million, or 10 million customers and to conduct a business with proper customer service. True, it's possible, but there are limitations to improving the customers' absolute satisfaction. This is because the administrative problems created by the large number of internal customers, or employees, are also serious. Large corporations attract many customers and generate sales at attractive prices. They're forced to hire a large number of employees to manage their many customers and another group of employees to manage their own employees. Companies are spending a considerable amount of money on human resources.

Furthermore, unless the monopoly is maintained, it's not easy to maximize the benefits while paying extra costs to keep the competition in check. Still, one startup owner who was opening his first company came to me, and he announced he'd create a million customers for his company. It's a great idea, of course, but the company should be able to fix the problems with good products. And the products should be accompanied by funding and many people to reach that stage. One prospective business owner said he could easily create a free application that could have one million downloads fast if the company had investors. He also said that it's a good product, but it's free, so it will be easy to reach that stage. Nonetheless, what about the server costs incurred by so many people, and what about the maintenance costs of making updates if the application is free? He said he could make a fortune from advertising installed in the application. However, some applications already offer similar services without advertising, so people don't have to use his application with annoying advertisements.

According to a 2016 global report from Appboy, only 11 percent of applications are reused after seven days and four percent after 90 days. However, there were so many prospective startup owners who thought they could make a fortune from advertising once their applications were downloaded by a large number of users. On the other hand, even among the more than one million downloaded applications, a large number of applications disappeared due to failure to generate further profits. It's not too late for many startup owners to say they will satisfy a large number of their customers with free and low-cost products after listening to the stories of the people who have failed in such projects.

There are many startup owners who have applications with a high number of application downloads but are not profitable. Many times they're worried because their application has high value but can't make them profitable, and the costs continue to rise. Also, a high number of downloads don't guarantee a good investment.

Customers should be satisfied with application usage, so if the company tries to lead them to the payment of the application, high satisfaction can minimize customer complaints. The number of downloads doesn't reflect the customers' loyalty. If the application fee is small but customers aren't satisfied, the requests for refunds will run continuously, and dealing with clients can be hectic. And since it's difficult to get over such a situation with a small number of people at the beginning of the company, the project can no longer be carried out by startups.

In this regard, startups must first make sure to satisfy a small number of customers. People are so sensitive to certain figures and grades that they try to appeal to customers and investors by creating all kinds of numbers that can disguise low sales. Whatever lies behind that, the time comes when you really need to make money and receive investments, and this will be disclosed all over the place. Therefore, startups need to keep their target customers narrow so that they can identify certain points in them that the customers were not previously satisfied with.

In other words, all you need to do is find a client who is willing to pay for your product, even if he or she is satisfied with only a particular part of it. Of course, there are few such vendors who target this way. Even if the price is relatively high, there are some places in these fringe markets where you can increase customer satisfaction. This is possible because you're targeting a very small number of customers. If you target many customers, it's difficult to manage the satisfaction level of individual customers. If you raise the price but cannot raise the customer satisfaction level, that's definitely a problem. However, raising prices and increasing customer satisfaction at the same time can never be a problem.

5. Six steps to expand customers as entrepreneurs of zero-base startups (startups with no capital).

Where and how do I find customers? For those of you who start a business, this is the biggest issue. And it's a part that's important in most of the business classes. Most businesspeople draw a sketch of their customers through persona analysis, which is typically targeted. And they analyze where such customers are most active. It's the way a typical startup works to provide feedback and promote upcoming products as well as how they conduct the product survey.

A zero-base startup specifies customers in a slightly different way. The first customer to be satisfied is the founder himself or herself. They ask themselves if it's a product or service that cheers them up as a customer. Some might ask, "Who has a business item that founders don't like in the first place?" But it's a slightly different point of view, depending on where the startup item started.

Usually, people are interested in problems that are found externally to create startup items. Since many people say that a particular situation is inconvenient, they say the demand for a particular market is high. They say that's to be expected of a particular industry soon, and they choose those items.

Entrepreneurs of zero-base startups have a slightly different start. They begin with the inconvenience the founder is experiencing in their own life. Or when their family has problems, the founder comes up with an item that solves an uncomfortable issue, and the engagement rate increases. So why not start with a problem found externally? It's also possible. That's because it's so closely linked to the founder's life that it can act as a problem. Whether the problem is from within or from without, the founder should be the first customer to benefit from his or her own products. Being the most enthusiastic customer, you can assume that you are leading the way in solving the problems.

The second level of the customer is hidden in the founder. The first customer is the one who thinks it's okay to fix the problem in any way possible because he or she is in urgent need. On the other hand, a second customer hidden in the founder is one who wants to solve the problem in a more flexible and sophisticated way.

For example, the founder can call on a more difficult customer who is hidden in the founder. The founder should feel satisfied when they look at something they don't normally feel comfortable with, and it's an item worth paying for. The process of satisfying the second customer, who is more demanding, must be carried out. Only then can the founder get a "wow" point when the next customer sees this.

There are no external factors to this process. There is only one standard, which is the founder herself or himself. Only when you are confident in your product can you confidently sell to other customers. Butterfly Investment was not satisfied with developing and providing one or two startup items, so it chose to give weekly item reports for one whole year[1].

The Coffee Club, which is cofounded with Butterfly Investment, has moved beyond simply providing dating events and made it possible to connect men

---

[1] The one of the main services of Butterfly Investment is developing and publishing new business items report weekly to its customers and let them select the business items and guide to start their own business with those items. Sometimes Butterfly Investment can have the stocks as a stock holder depending the guidance level. And if they don't' want to start the business yet, BI can guide them to change the view of starting the business as Zero base startup

and women and enable them to talk about life without knowing each other's background. Coomm Life Games (https://100daysgame.modoo.at/), which is also cofounded with Butterfly Investment, has chosen to write more than 100 books with 100 people altogether. Each has "wow" points.

The third level of the customer comprises the friends and acquaintances who surround the founder. People often say that business is difficult and should not be conducted with acquaintances. Selling to an acquaintance when the founder is unsure about the products and services he or she sells will, of course, cause problems. However, if it's a product that's useful to an acquaintance, and the founder is confident enough to explain its value without hesitation, it's not a bad thing to sell the product to friends.

I read in the news that some people took Western medicine for diet but had side effects. If I'm a Western doctor who makes Western medicine properly, and my friend takes Western medicine that has side effects, I should prevent my friend from taking that medicine. And then shouldn't I encourage them to find and eat safe herbal medicines? If an acquaintance believes in the wrong information but you don't correct them, he or she will continue to believe in the wrong information and take low-value drugs that have side effects.

If you're a business founder who's confident about providing products and services to clients, you don't have to be afraid of selling them to your acquaintances.

The fourth level of the customer is not acquaintances but strangers. The founder can sell a product to a stranger because the founder has previously sold it to acquaintances for a certain price. And since the founder received constructive feedback from the acquaintances after the sales, the founder is also able to sell to strangers in a more sophisticated fashion.

The fifth level involves standardizing and institutionalizing the process of sales so it's conducted to the public but still is a person-to-person process. Sales comments, product descriptions, and customer questions can be set up and elaborated on. Since it's still a full-time job to meet clients one by one, the company is able to handle small groups of customers and treat them as VIP customers who are familiar with the company and recognize its products and services and make up for the lack of customer service.

Because they still have a person-to-person process of selling and don't carry out massive marketing campaigns, the founder can still directly respond to possible customer complaints. That's because the company will maintain the satisfaction level of its initial customers and early adopters so they do the viral marketing by themselves. Many startup companies make the mistake of only posting on social networking sites as viral marketing. But this practice comes from a big misunderstanding. When even a small number of customers are truly satisfied, and when they report their products to their close friends and family, true viral marketing has begun.

The sixth level is a group of customers who spontaneously increase through word of mouth between the customers. It's a difficult process to persuade a customer who's a total stranger, and while there are barriers to making sales, it's simpler and more natural for a customer to persuade other customers. With this, the satisfaction level is also high.

The customers you'll meet in step seven are public. Once the founder has gathered the response of the sixth customer, the product will now have a quality and brand that will fully appeal to prospective customers who have watched the product for a long time. From this point on, both the customer base and the fan base can increase quickly, and the company can expand in size.

Even without any effort, it's the phase during which requests for press releases, publications, and interviews are received. The circumstances we've experienced so far are reflected in those stages. Among misunderstanding and lack of information, we set up Butterfly Investment and created the case to spread the spirit of business without capital. We've encountered a handful of customers and have continued to delay massive online promoting.

Butterfly Investment keeps creating successful businesses started without any capital, zero-base startups, and developed a good fan base. As a brand, Butterfly Investment has grown, so people who weren't interested in starting a business now also wonder about Butterfly Investment's products. And Butterfly Investment reached the point where we have clients who weren't interested in startups purchase our services anyway to learn about our system.

Word has spread that people can get inspiration even if they're not entrepreneurs, learn useful tips that can be used at work, and witness people who build their own brands at work after they met Butterfly Investment. In addition, if people are really interested in starting a business without any money, then they come to Butterfly Investment to receive special motivational training materials before they become entrepreneurs and start their businesses.

From the beginning, amazing things have happened for Butterfly Investment. And I find it astonishing to have a diverse group of clients throughout the country and abroad. Butterfly Investment and other companies that have been in business together for two to three years are also experiencing this phase.

The first customer is the founder herself or himself, but as the founder moves up slowly, the number of customers increases. Yet founders from Butterfly Investment spend very little on media and marketing. They can market whenever they want, but they don't have to because good word of mouth brings them more customers.

If founders had invested heavily in marketing from the beginning in search of customers from the outside, they would have relied on it for a long time and would not have survived in the long run. Keep that in mind. Starting small and making sales through feedback and improvements can make a company survive longer.

6. Why Butterfly Investment insists on pre-sales.

"I get paid before the product is completed. Then I make products and set up the company with that money from pre-sales." This has become a natural process for me. Butterfly Investment is set up this way, and all Butterfly Investment cofounded companies are set up this way too. Many people agree that it makes sense to start dozens of companies this way, but they don't think they can start such a business by themselves.

I can understand their mindset, because I didn't take it for granted that I could start my own business this way either. I only followed the guidance of Choi, who shared the same message with the public to spread the way in which they could start their businesses without any capital to avoid any failure. As we faced each other in the field, we became more confident in how we started our new businesses, as we became more complete with the idea of making sales and growing recognized startups.

Then, did Choi start his career this way from the beginning? No. He's also been mentioned in the previous co-written book *The Pirates' Startup Story*. He received a large amount of money from various investors and grew his business through fierce competition. And he went as far as to pay employees using private loans with high interests fees.

He wasn't aware of the importance of the zero-base startup in the beginning. He experienced firsthand how unhappy it would be if the life of the founder were ruined in the end because he tried to solve problems with money alone. He grew his business on the strength of money. Nonetheless, he felt skeptical about the way he started the business and felt the necessity of starting a business without any capital (zero-base startup) when he and other prominent businesspeople around him hit the bottom of their lives.

He started his own business by saying, "You must not touch large amounts of money unless you embody sales, and you must create sales without relying on money." Butterfly Investment established and operated a company with money from pre-sales. He had great confidence in the business process that occurs through pre-sales, and I'll introduce some of the experiences that have strengthened that conviction.

The first case is a home shopping story that shows the power of pre-sales. Choi told a story about starting a business from home shopping without inventory. With only one sample product that could be shown on the air, he could sell products to clients. It was easier then to introduce products to home shopping than now. Choi experimented with one electronic product and received orders in large quantities. Of course, he had no inventory on hand. The orders had flooded in; he had to deliver the products. With this pre-selling situation on hand, Choi searched for agents and dealers and negotiated the prices. He requested better terms because he would place a large order.

How did the dealerships respond? They couldn't refuse the offer on the confirmed orders. Eventually, he was able to make a favorable contract with the dealers for a better offer and delivered the goods to customers.

Wholesale dealers buy a lot of things at once, so they get them at a low price. Choi was not a wholesale merchant who purchased large quantities of goods in advance, but a wholesale merchant who sold them to consumers in advance and used the money to buy the products later. I think in the common business scenario, the owner orders the products in bulk first with his own money and sells them to consumers.

However, Choi came to realize the power of pre-sales when he took orders from consumers in advance and found a wholesaler to offer them later. If entrepreneurs go to the market first without a business foundation, there are many limitations to the negotiations. But if entrepreneurs have a client in advance to buy the products, in other words, if you put sales first, you'll gain an advantage in negotiations with your counterparties. With pre-sales, it's possible to offer cheaper products to customers and to help business owners make big sales at once while reducing the inventory burden.

He made sure there were no unresolved problems in the business in this way. At first, he made a deal with one of the biggest company's headquarters, which had initially rejected the deal, and secured the bank to proceed with the transactions in a way it had never done before.

His sales experiments continued. When he ran a shopping mall years ago, he also found a lucrative business deal and partners through pre-sales. While handing out flyers on the street for pre-sales, he received an order for the lowest-priced electronic products. That way, he made 100-million-won worth of sales in advance, he went to negotiate with dealers with that order statement, and made a profit even though he sold the products at lower than the minimum price from internet market. Then he started a shopping mall business with that profit. The online shopping mall, which sold 100 million won without its homepage, opened an opportunity for investors to invest and to lend money, so it grew rapidly.

The School Monster makes a profit from the lectures and seminars, and it's also based on the pre-sales mechanism. A typical lecture/seminar agent and management company seeks a well-known lecturer or speaker equipped with a lecture plan, and also owns and runs the lecture room or big auditorium. There are costs that are basically incurred before the customer comes. On the other hand, before the lecture curriculum is complete, School Monster puts up a lecture/seminar introduction and a table of contents online first. It means that they sell the lecture tickets first. Of course, there are some lectures/seminars that aren't popular. Then School Monster (http://www.schoolmonster.kr) changes the title of the seminar to make it even more interesting, and he also revisits the lecture introduction so that people would like to buy it because it's more fashionable.

If he repeats this process, he'll have someone paying for the lecture. With the number of students who already bought the tickets, it's inevitable to complete the lecture curriculum quickly. Lecturers won't need to worry about not selling the tickets anymore. They can complete a lecture that was already sold.

Choi said he felt confident in this method because he continued to test zero-base startups by selling like this and then specifying products and services.

So when Butterfly Investment started selling business-idea documents relating to zero-base startups, we had to stick to the pre-sales strategy. We didn't produce the documents in advance. We didn't even make the company homepage in advance. We started selling the services right away. Of course, it was a strange way for me, and I would have given it up if Choi had not led me. When we were selling, people looked suspicious, and I couldn't answer their questions at first. I had previously experienced the sales process while selling insurance, but the cold stare of the people was still hard for me to endure.

Nevertheless, I imagined how well this business would go in the future, how fewer people would go bankrupt, how fewer people would become homeless, and how fewer social crimes would be committed after Butterfly Investment spread the spirit of zero- base startups. Then I got my own sales mentors, built the sales processes, gained self-confidence, and got my clients who paid.

Instead of making and selling documents for the idea of starting a business without any capital (zero-base startup) beforehand, the company started to make them and deliver them every week after the customer completed the payment. So I started making documents every week after getting paid in advance. At first, the accumulation speed was slow. I have produced and delivered without failure for the past year, two years, three years and four years. Documents, videos, lectures, and co-founders associated with Butterfly Investment have grown exponentially and have come to the point where they're automatically generating online sales. There are still many misunderstandings about starting a business without any capital, and I'm faithfully playing a role to resolve them and also to warn people who recklessly start a business based on trust in money. Butterfly Investment makes a profit out of these inspiring documents and videos, which allows it to create cofounded companies with people who are inside of us. All of the cofounded companies with Butterfly Investment are based solely on this pre-sales system. And the founder also makes a contract not to receive investments and loans from others.

Butterfly Investment has maintained this tradition since it was founded. If founders sell products to a customer first and have money to produce the product, they have a better way or even a better deal to produce the product afterwards, which then occurs under favorable terms. If a founder can't sell the products to a customer first, the founder will be insecure about the product and service, and will naturally want to stop selling the products.

I'm well aware of what to worry about when new entrepreneurs hear about pre-sales. "What if there's a situation in which you don't give in and fail to make what you have agreed to make, and what if you're branded as a fraud?" That kind of horror comes from pre-sales.

Therefore, you should never sell a product unless you're confident and willing to keep your promises to clients.

In fact, you don't know what you are until you actually try to sell your products first. You can find out your real ability by selling, and see if you might have a tendency to cheat customers. Many people grow up by selling and organizing their pre-sales, build content, and turn into wonderful and unexpected business people. There are some people who seemed to be really good at business, but they didn't manage it after the pre-sales, and they alienate their clients. Of course, I always talk to such people. I tell them, "You're going the way of the con artist, and it's too dangerous." The person who admits it is likely to get the job done well by apologizing or returning to the customer. And the person who ignores it disconnects from me and reveals their limitations by revealing their own way.

That's why I continue to emphasize in my documents and videos the importance of self-organizing and the importance of good values. Through the pre-sales process, a strong person becomes stronger, and a wicked person reveals his or her evils more quickly. Before creating larger problems, there's a chance to control them. Otherwise, beginning entrepreneurs can have more money and damage more people.

Pre-sales are more than just getting paid in advance from customers and making a lucrative contract with a client. They show the limits of the founder and provide a springboard to entrepreneurship. They give people self-knowledge and prevent them from starting their own business recklessly. I've done that in the past, and I'll continue to develop my founders in the future and make sure every prospective entrepreneur in the world starts with pre-sales naturally.

7. Break the stereotypes of pre-sales first.

You may still be skeptical about making pre-sales when the product is incomplete or when it's not available yet. Few people start their business this way. Even those who started a zero-base startup at first felt strange about this method. However, creating sales and sales channels first is not the only way in the world. We've seen a lot of other ways all around us.

For instance, consider the case of people buying a house as an installment sale for a builder building new homes. People pay a deposit even though their house is not built yet. It's like paying first. And once the money is collected, the builder begins to build a house with an additional loan.

The intermediate funds come in again, and contractors finish the construction again. The company doesn't take the client's money after building a house with the company's funds. Clients pay a few thousand to several hundred million won first, the company builds the house with those funds, and then clients finally get a house.

Some people who learned about Butterfly Investment's new zero-base startup business model also asked, "Where's an example of a company that makes products with funds from pre-sales?" However, many people bought houses this way already. They're willing to pay a large sum of money to buy a house that isn't built yet.

There are more examples that can be interpreted as using the pre-sales method. You may have heard of crowdfunding. Literally, it's to be funded by the public to make an offer products and services with that money. WADIZ and Tumblebug are famous crowdfunding sites in Korea.

They feature a sophisticated introduction to upcoming works and services by artists, writers, and entrepreneurs, and sell their products in advance. If the money exceeds the amount agreed upon, the money can be used to make the products and offer them to the people involved. There is certainly a risk as the crowdfunding companies are raising money only on promises. That's why there are often times when people are involved in funding for a price benefit or extra products.

Those who trust and pay before the product hits the market are worth VIP treatment. In this way, crowdfunding is also a way to grow a business by selling its products first. Crowdfunding sites like Kickstarter and Indiegogo are also popular, and many companies launch their projects through these sites. They seduce customers by providing them with a stylish introduction to the products to be created and why they are made, and prototypes and benefits for them on their crowdfunding web page.

I have many products from crowdfunding projects and most of them are satisfying. "Who in the world starts a business with pre-sales?" I've been asked. But if you look around, you'll find that there are already many people who have started a business this way. Nevertheless, I thought about the reasons they would challenge the concept of a zero-base startup beginning with pre-sales.

First, it seems impossible to take responsibility after the sales.

If they sold products in advance, but it would be too burdensome to take follow-up responsibility after that, they could not make pre-sales. Therefore, when they make a perfect product first and are proud of it, then they want to sell it. That's how I would do it if I could produce goods that everybody is satisfied with, with an abundance of funds. But that's not the case.

Investment and money must continue to come in to make products perfect. Creating a product that will please everybody will miss the timing to launch. If you want to avoid the situation in which all these resources are invested but fail in the end, you must start a business in a way that sells a product first and prepares it later.

Second, they think they're hearing a con artist or swindler.

This is what I'm most concerned about, and so are other new founders. If you sell a product and don't take responsibility and do not deliver the product, you deserve to be called a fraud. Seeing what you don't want to be responsible for, you should realize, "I'll have to stay alert and do business right." Or further think, "I should not do business."

Smart friends who are only interested in making money with their overflowing enthusiasm make many of these mistakes. Many people mistakenly believe that they know everything about what they've learned, and sell on the basis of what they've learned from a textbook.

Occasionally, a founder may not be able to keep their initial promise. At this time, they can compensate customers with more goods and services than they actually expected; however, avoiding customers makes founders frauds, of course.

Third, they're afraid to look bad. Everyone would be interested in starting a business with a large number of employees in a sparkly office, and also in selling products that are highly resilient. However, some people build up to that point, and others do not.

When a person who has not yet matured enough wants to be recognized and decides to start a business, it's a mistake to borrow a large amount of money and receive investments first. When you start a business without money, you have the opportunity to meet your limitations quickly and grow as you reach them, but when you have money, you're just covering up limitations with money.

It's scary to be out in front of people when you're not ready. In the beginning, you must face your fear, and even you must love it. Early on, overcoming what seemed to be insurmountable problems makes it easier and more interesting to start a business. If you don't show up in the beginning, you'll lose the chance to love your real self.

My initiative is to start a business with sales and to fund the operations of the business with sales only. This method is not entirely new. What already existed in the world has been adapted and refined for today's business creator.

People think it goes against common sense because it's an unfamiliar way of doing business. Beyond concerns about common sense, you think of the business as pyramid selling or as a false idea. This is a limited interpretation within that framework of pyramid selling.

I'm also used to this reaction. I understand the feelings of those who respond this way.

However, I would like to ask once again if the method I pursue is truly out of the realm of common sense.

Think carefully about whether you've ever been a pre-sales customer for someone in real life. I'd like to ask you if you ever paid before the product was made or before the service began. It's not unusual to start a business with pre-sales. It's very common to grow by selling to a small number of customers.

By the way, what do we think is the common sense idea of starting a business? Is it ever common sense to take a big investment that's way out of your league, get a huge loan from the bank, get into a business with fierce competition, and then go bankrupt? A founder must discover their limitations through the zero-base startup method, and create their own vessel that can handle money as they grow.

8. Five points to make pre-sales successful.

Most of the new business owners who are now making progress with Butterfly Investment had never learned about the concept of pre-sales before. They met various concepts I created under the keyword "zero-base startup," and after gaining inspiration for the sales experience, they started to make sales easily. Some people get dramatic results right after they get to know some of the key messages I deliver about zero-base startups. Other people are envious of them. And then they feel uncomfortable about why they don't get sales so soon.

One of the most difficult questions I've ever asked was, "How soon have you settled down after you started your own business?" It's the question that is most likely to be asked. However, it's difficult to answer this question because people don't know the answer.

When I'm asked these questions, I must ask them again:

"What have you done to start your own business?"

"How many people will support you when you start a business?"

"How many hours a day can you actually sell the product in front of people?"

"Can you attend our seminar every week?"

"Are you confident in participating in the mission?"

"What exactly does it mean to be 'settled down'?"

You have to answer these questions first so I can explain them further.

Instead, I'm going to tell you what's different about the challenges people face when starting a zero-base startup business, and creating sales and high revenue streams.

So from now on, I'll talk about the five conditions under which sales are made. Of course, it's now possible to quickly start building up these conditions if you accept that you don't have these conditions and think about learning new ones.

First, they've already built up trust.

When a company worker decides to quit his job and start his own business, how does he or she behave in the company before leaving the office?

"Now that I'm quitting, I'll come and go from work as I want. I don't want to see them anyway after I leave." Or, "They might be my potential buyers or clients, so I should be responsible and leave a good impression until the end of the day."

I want you to look back on how you finished your last days at a company or are likely to do so. The characteristic of people who have established trust is that they think and behave as in the latter example. There's no chance to test the trust in good times.

You have a chance to build trust by what you do after a relationship ends or things go sour. It's hard to trust a person who's forfeited their integrity if their interests are removed. There are some people who have done so in the past and done it this way every time.

When they say they're starting their own business, it's not easy to attract support as well as sales. You never know when you'll be good or bad if you actually start a business. But those who have built up trust are expected to do well in the end. This makes it possible to generate pre-sales volume even if there are only a few products and explanations at the beginning stage of the project.

Second, they have their own brand to generate pre-sales.

You may have heard a lot about the importance of branding. There are also many ways to make your own branding. However, I think the essence of branding is maintaining it for the long run. Someone who already has much experience in one field may have their own brand in the field or may have it easily soon. Personal branding can be created this way without someone being a renowned author or lecturer. I've met several experts who are familiar with one field, through an application called http://taling.me. This is a famous application for connecting talents or experts and people who want to learn. In this application, college students are able to earn money by tutoring in subjects other than their majors, such as composing or guitar lessons.

How do college students form their own branding as specialists in areas not related to their majors? Moreover, how do they get money in advance? People can check their portfolios. When you look at the portfolios, even if the subjects are not their majors, they have practiced and performed them for more than 10 years since childhood, so you can't help acknowledging their expertise. It's different from people who cram for tests and get a certificate in a short period of time. The time they spend on their expertise makes their own branding. And people see this and appreciate the tutors' branding as specialists in their own fields. Therefore, they make payment first through the application and meet with them to get private tutoring. I have never regretted taking such classes.

Even though someone is starting their own business now, they've often developed their favorite hobby for a long time, and then make a quick sale by making good use of it. They have invested their time in their own personal branding. So people who don't spend that time don't have to be envious of their accomplishments.

Third, there is the charm.

It's not just about appearance. I read an article saying that comedians are good at dating and marrying regardless of their appearance. I attribute this to charm. Humor is also a kind of charm. There's a person whose charm comes across when they meet someone. There's no explosiveness in the speech, and they're a good listener. Gestures and eye contact that are considerate of others also add to the charm. Well-groomed hair, a bright voice, and a bright smile increase the charm. People like this have the advantage of making sales. It's something they've learned from themselves over the years.

"He looks like a fraud; don't you think?" You may think so. Yes. Well-trained crooks know that people pay easily when they meet attractive sellers. However, they don't have the first or second point described above. Anyone who has risen to the point of attraction without the first and second points stated in the paragraph above could be on a blacklist. It's important to increase the attractiveness. This is because it's likely to slow down the sales performance when the founder has the first and second point mentioned above but misses this point.

Fourth, there's passion and conviction in the founder.

I tend to be wary of boundless enthusiasm and conviction. While we respect such energy, this is a prejudice created from the experience of burning quickly and cooling easily. (Of course, I've burnt myself out a few times.) There's a reason for calling it prejudice. It's because one in 100 people have a constant outpour of such pure enthusiasm and conviction.

There's definitely a person who repeats the challenges of recklessness and continues to draw enthusiasm even after a failure. It's far from the thrill of meeting just new things, and the feeling of passion that comes with it. There's a kind of person who burns like a torch that won't go out, and I'm seeing some of them close by in business now.

Such a person seems like they hold a diamond. They're not flashy yet they reveal their inner brilliance. Even if it doesn't work out, I still want to be with them. I'm willing to be their first customer when they start a new business.

In a way, it's a part that can also be associated with charm, but it's distinct from the charm described above. Rather, they feel less sophisticated. That's why I'm saying it's like holding a diamond. If they study how to apply their charm a little bit, they can continuously create a sales pitch and a fan base who can become regular clients.

Fifth, just go for it.

Obviously, a person who keeps trying "to sell first, produce later" makes a profit in the end. If you're not attractive as a businessperson yet, or you don't have the brand yet so you keep postponing sales, the opportunity to sell the products continues to drift away. No one knows, in fact, how much appeal and trust can bring sales. A founder breaks down repeatedly, builds trust with clients without realizing it, and turns into a real businessperson. People who regularly stand up will step over the wall of pre-sales faster than they think.

Because there are so many different customer groups in the world, there are definitely some customers who don't buy a product because they're not told to buy it even if they are ready to pay for it. Of course, such clients can be met by active founders who try to stand in front of clients several times. A passive founder can never meet such a client.

Therefore, we should not be envious of the person who makes pre-sales right after they started, even though they don't have various product lines. That's because they tried to put a lot of effort into meeting clients.

It's only natural that a person with these five qualifications should make a big sale as soon as they receive guidance from Butterfly Investment and me about the zero-base startup. People who have tried to start a new business without having these characteristics should be prepared to develop these qualities. When you're aware of your current status, you're able to study and to make truly transformative efforts.

"How soon do you succeed when you try to a zero-base startup?" Before asking the question, look at the information above and ask how much you've invested in those qualifications. Start by acknowledging your shortcomings and then make tight schedules to change yourself. Then, you can answer this question on your own.

9. Why a six-digit income isn't so difficult for anyone to achieve.

The symbolic number of the successful annual salary is 100 million won or $100,000. Even if you work for a large company, it takes a while to make 100 million won, excluding tax. People who quit their jobs and start their own business also target 100 million won in profits. So, first, a prospective founder starts a business by searching for items that can make a fortune. To make a big sales revenue, people choose popular items as well as cheap ones. There seems to be no logic in making this choice. However, the reality after starting a business is completely different from what we expected.

Having to deal with a large number of customers requires a large number of employees; therefore, big labor costs are set aside for sales if it's a retail business. This will apply to other business models too. As I mentioned earlier, although labor costs are high to manage 100,000 to one million users by developing applications, high server costs may force a business to close. When you say that one million people have downloaded free applications, you need to distinguish between the excellent application services that resulted in word-of-mouth downloads or just the short-term results from the reckless marketing with high costs incurred to make sure the applications are downloaded.

With so many users of the application, it's not easy to keep up with the clients' requests or to update the program regularly. Even the famous writers and entrepreneurs who came to my business consulting program were suffering from similar problems.

People who think they have a large number of fans are more likely to gather a large number of users or clients of their services to make money. When they start their business, they realize that they have more work to do than they expected and that they don't know what to do with their labor and maintenance costs. Even if money is continuously invested, money is soon dried up, customer satisfaction isn't elevated, communication with employees is difficult, and the founder experiences the bitter taste of running a business. Even if the company produces $1million of revenue in this way, it's not easy for the founder to receive $100,000 as their own before taxes.

One entrepreneur whom I met in the consulting program also complained that he could not keep $100,000 in hand running a big company, despite making sales revenue of up to $10 million in a year. The same is true of self-employed people. How much money do you think the owner of a convenience store that makes $30,000 a month will get for himself or herself? I've seen a news article related to this. Of course, it was mentioned as a worst case scenario, but the owner received as salary $1,000 less than the part-time employee who worked for their store.

In fact, I heard this story from some of the owners of convenience stores who came to my startup lecture; they said the case mentioned above is the reality. They said the owner intentionally managed multiple convenience stores at the same time, but it's difficult to manage them all and doesn't work well.

I continue to emphasize in this that if you think you'll succeed in business with a strategy that makes you generate a large number of customers at a low price, you'll most likely be very frustrated in front of a cold reality. But you'll start to wonder why I said a six-digit income a year is not a difficult one to achieve. That's based on my story as well as a story from people around me, and it's the way the entrepreneurs of zero-base startups are going now.

Entrepreneurs of zero-base startups don't start businesses with the idea of creating 100,000 to one million customers at a time. With the idea of starting by creating 1,000 enthusiastic customers, they operate their businesses and gradually increase the number of customers. In one example, the clients share many similarities with the entrepreneurs of a startup company. It's a service built for people who have issues in common with entrepreneurs, and people who are in a similar position become clients and expect the service to work well. The love and affection for services and products are totally different from the people who use it only because it's free.

Let's talk about the business case from Butterfly Investment that's running the business with a relatively small customer target. There are many dating match services both online and offline, but most of those services reveal personal information when they match people. However, some people realize that, when they meet someone while making the most of the details revealed, prejudice is created because of this information. And also they realize that this detailed information hides the truth from each other. However, there was no service in existence for those people who do not wish to know the background of their date before they met. In this regard, The Coffee Club made such a service. Of course, Kim, Yoon, CEO of The Coffee Club, also had similar thoughts before she launched her business. Therefore, she has made the services for clients who have the same problems as the people who want to solve it proactively.

Few people are aware of such unusual problems, but they certainly exist. Moreover, there are fewer people who are willing to deal with them at high costs. There will be 1,000 more of them in the world.

Many people started their businesses by making large investments and taking out big loans but eventually experienced the scary side of money and people. They realized that psychology, attitude, and emotional management are more important than money. I realize how much energy is wasted by fierce competition, and it's not important to have just a high sales rate.

For those of you who want to get the know-how of failed and resilient entrepreneurs, pay for Butterfly Investment and become a customer. Their goal is to create 1,000 customers first to solve certain problems. Even if such a customer pays only $10 a month, it's worth $10,000 a month in total. If the service costs $100, it's $100,000 a month.

If you take advantage of the free online community to manage about 1,000 people, you don't have to have many employees. Many people who come to my startup beginner class refer to one million users first. Then, I tell them to keep in mind only 1,000 people and to prepare for the service first. Then the problem is simpler than they thought. Instead, they can make authentic content, conduct regular lectures and seminars related to the service, and create social networking services to enable such clients to discover their services and attract them. Such clients don't respond to poor marketing or tricks.

When professional marketers promote applications and add users, they may receive $1 or $2 for each new user. Nonetheless, how many users would be needed for genuine promotion? When one million people download a certain application, it will also be promoted under the title "One Million Download Application," but how many users will actually be happy and willing to pay for the company and service?

Think about the 1,000 people willing to pay for the service and product and focus on making such services. Create high-quality content and promote it with the utmost determination to find them. Remove other customers from the list of concerns for now.

What if we could get 1,000 ideal customers like that? There are many options at this stage. Among these customers, you can find a business partner and create another service together. If you've found a small group of congenial employees and business partners while you have 1,000 customers, then you can slowly achieve 10,000 customers, or even 100,000 customers while you grow supporting 1,000 people.

In the process of creating 1,000 loyal customers, the founder discovers all of his or her potentials and deficiencies. In that situation, I would like to tell the founder to decide the future of the company. Of course, I wouldn't choose to get any investment from outside. I would continue to support the startups that are creating 1,000 customers and have a mission to guide them not to be invested at that stage.

Remember that. One day you'll be contented with one million people by starting your own business. But not right now. Now, you only have to run with 1,000 customers who are loyal to the service you've created and who are willing to pay $10 a month. This alone is enough to achieve a six-digit income a year.

If you have a pleasant businessperson around you who makes over $100,000 a year running a fun business, it's more likely that he or she is familiar with the secret. Knowing this secret and collecting revenue based on pre-sales will give you a free life while you earn a six-digit income.

10. Find a partner who really can do sales.

I have a valuable partner. He taught me how to start a new business as a zero-base startup. He is Mr. Choi Gyu-Cheol, and he is a coauthor of my previous book—*The Pirates' Startup Story*—and co-founder of Butterfly Investment as well. If it hadn't been for this man, I wouldn't have started my own business. I tried hard to do sales before, but I was also more motivated by the fact that he showed me how to sell in advance.

Sometimes an investor is called a business partner, but entrepreneurs of zero-base startups don't have such business partners as we don't receive any investments. People who can generate synergies with the sale are considered partners. Butterfly Investment's business ideas also prioritizes first the founder's ability to form a company as well as sales with Butterfly Investment.

Although it's generally mentioned in the book, the ability to sell is not affected only by skills. The love of products, enthusiasm to carry out business despite concerns, and sincerity all lead to sales ability. At least someone who loves the company's products deserves to be

CEO, and this is the kind of person to consider creating a partnership with.

In the early stage, the fear and loneliness of starting one's own business should not be used to decide on a partnership with anyone visible to you. If you're considering a partnership with someone you've met at a time when you have an opportunity to talk about business, someone you owe, or a close friend with whom you've talked about business, make sure you consider the following.

First, clearly define the equity or company stake with your partners.

It's very ambiguous to define a stake in the early stage of business between close friends. It doesn't seem to be very compatible with Korean emotions to talk about such figures. Nevertheless, it's quite right to draw the line and talk clearly about the shareholding ratio. Moreover, the person leading the initial direction of business should have more shares.

Zero-base startups may not be relevant in their initial equity holdings as they start with a small capital, but it's necessary for those who are determined to carry on the project and company to the end to ensure they have more stake and share. The leading side should show such determination and power of sales. Therefore, it's highly recommended to set up a certain number of initial business models first, set up a structure to sell products, and then hire a partner. That way, there are fewer conflicts in the initial equity shareholding. When you start painting a picture jointly with a partner from the start of the business, you're also very concerned about sharing your shares, and it's also difficult to gain speed in the process of doing business. Furthermore, when you need to speed up the growth of your business, it usually slows down as conflicts repeat with your partners who have a stake in the company.

Second, it's necessary to motivate the partner.

At the beginning of the project, the person who drives the direction of business should have a large number of shares. That way, the company has less trouble moving forward at the beginning. If you select a partner who's interested in the business, you should motivate him or her in a way that gives them some shares, and later you can give more based on his or her contribution to the business overall.

It's not possible to motivate a partner through equity if he or she is evenly distributed from the beginning. When democracy and equality are uncritically applied to business, it's difficult to achieve goals jointly through business startups.

There are values that will apply differently over time to the organization, business, and group are shaped.

Those values should be applied with a little expression of empathy as possible. You shouldn't apply the same emotions to your business that you experience in your daily personal life.

It's the business that should be careful of "a blessing in disguise." It's the business that makes the worst of the "good things" situation. When a business principle exists, and a contract is signed to abide by it, choices are then made based on the contract and not on emotion.

The person who says "yes" to all is a person who doesn't know business. When you meet such a person, don't even think about joining hands with him as a business partner. They're more likely to care only about profitable allocation than business feasibility and vision. In severe cases, they'll be the first to quit when business is slow, and if the business is successful, they'll show an over-the-top ambition.

Third, validate the partner through sales capacity.

Not only the partner but also the person to be hired as an employee should be verified by sales capacity. At least, even if they aren't good at selling yet, they should understand the importance of sales within the company and have no objection to practicing. Wouldn't it be odd to choose a partner or employee who isn't able to talk about the products the company sells?

I went to a meeting where I met an employee who spoke proudly about his company's products. All of a sudden, trust in the company rose dramatically. However, if people hide their company's products and don't speak up, you won't have any reason to believe in their company. Being able to sell the product is basically love or affection for the company. No one would like to work with a partner or an employee who has no love or passion for the company.

The partner is the one after the founder who has the ability to destroy the company. This is especially true if he or she has a large stake. It's the biggest reason why we have to choose a partner who has affection for the company. If the partner doesn't have any love or loyalty for the company, they won't hesitate to choose to destroy the company in the end. Therefore, you must be very careful in choosing a partner and giving them authority.

Butterfly Investment also has a very difficult process for finding a partner and setting up a company together. Potential partners should understand the system of salespreneurship through the Butterfly Investment membership program, and we go through a long process to understand each other as business partners. It's fundamental to verify the partner's capacity through sales performance. Reviewing how they run the company, Butterfly Investment provides the partner with a small stake first, and then keeps monitoring the partner and allocates more shares after that.

The same method applied when I established Butterfly Investment jointly with Choi. I started with fewer shares because I had to learn the basics from him, but I worked hard to sell and to promote the brand of the company. I was beginning to prove my contribution to the company with concrete sales performance and company branding. Later on, this led to me having more shares of Butterfly Investment.

There's a person who runs the business in the early stage, and then there's a runner-up who takes the lead in the later stage. If you don't take these steps into account, you distribute shares recklessly, or you take a business partner because he or she is your close friend. It's more likely that they will quit the business after suffering from the conflict between partners.

In fact, I've heard that one of the people who started a consulting business might suggest an ideal scenario, even though they don't have any experience at all between partners and don't feel bad about this. It's also likely you've been told to split the stake so that it looks equal between partners at 49:51. If you have someone who tells you this, make sure you check to see if he or she is a field salesperson, has any real business experience, or has a history of failing and resuming business. For those who come to my lectures, I keep saying that the reality of starting a business is not romantic and doesn't work ideally. A partner should never be easily acquired and should be verified by sales capacity. This is a bare minimum of validation. I want you to think about this calmly as you decide on your partner.

11. Sell intangible products first for real sales.

As I continue to give lectures on business startups, I meet people who have diverse ideas about startups. As a matter of fact, since the early stage of startups, I was usually selling intangible products or digital products, and I had some distance from the manufacturing industry. Then, a business selling suits and wallets were launched with Butterfly Investment and started a joint business mainly with items that are a combination of manufacturing and intangible services. This gave me a better understanding of the manufacturing industry. Nevertheless, I found that quite a few people who came to the lectures didn't know about manufacturing or felt it had nothing to do with the sale of intangible items. To start the manufacturing industry, they said they needed a factory check, a place to distribute, or a 3D printer for business. I continue to mention this in this book: The manufacturing industry can also sell first to produce and manufacture and offer products with that money. Zero-base startups don't distinguish between product types that are tangible versus intangible.

This chapter will tell you about the many opportunities to make money even if it's not from the manufacturing industry. There's a whole range of product parts overseas called *digital products*. In Korea, e-books, video lectures, applications, and web applications (such as logging in from the web, using services, and paying for costs) can all be classified as digital products.

Digital products also have the advantage of being inexpensive to produce, and they cost less than non-digital products to distribute. In addition to these sales, I also encourage people who have made incremental gains with digital products, as I did. It's easy to sell intangible products such as lectures, coaching, and electronic documents through a website called Kmong (www.kmong.com) in Korea. More members of the Butterfly Investment membership are expected to brand and profit from Kmong in the future.

My previously published book, *The Pirate's Startup Story*, was already sold as an e-book version before the paper book came out. The electronic book was also given to the reader as a digital product after I received payment in advance. My regular startup seminars— "The Pirate's Startup Story," "The Magic of Nothing," and "Sales is First"—are all filmed and sold on video clips first. These have been around for about two years, and the video lectures are also making monthly profits. Once a video clip is filmed and distributed through a certain platform, it's a comfortable source of passive income since someone simply has to be paid for it when it's sold through a video distribution company. There are no labor costs or upfront costs.

Currently, under Butterfly Investment, ZeroBizCampus (www.zerobizcampus.com), ran by Mr. Park Jong-moon, is providing various video lectures and coaching program created by founders and members of Butterfly Investment. Through this website, Butterfly Investment members are making their debut as instructors in Butterfly Investment. ZeroBizCampus is still collecting more video clips and lectures actively, and more and more people will come and start watching video lectures there.

There are many cases of people finding business items, becoming founders of companies and instructors or lecturers in certain fields, and selling video programs through Butterfly Investment.

More and more companies are offering video services online these days.

Such a business system is called the Learning Management System (LMS), and it offers education through online media—video, text, PowerPoint, and more. The LMS is already popular and actively utilized overseas.

You can also find lectures from famous universities online. Opportunities to buy online classes that can't be easily learned offline are increasing.

The number of Korean companies offering such services has also been on the rise for three to four years. Now they're offering English language video clips on overseas sites and creating sales opportunities.

If you want to sell the video online, don't just consider shooting the entire video. Guide videos describing the lecture may need to be produced for free or edited separately to stimulate curiosity. Once you film and start to sell your lectures online, passive income from the online lectures will come no matter what hours you work on weekdays. Of course, you can also promote yourself and build up your brand through online classes.

"It's a great idea, but I'm very afraid of showing my face publicly, and I don't like it."

Of course, there are tips for people who are afraid to show up. If you use PowerPoint and make videos, you can make a great video clip and an online lecture. When I first started my YouTube channel, Zero Startup (Zero︎︎), which I've been running for years, I used to try this kind of video at the beginning. It wasn't easy for me to come forward and speak at the beginning. So I put the PowerPoint slides on the computer screen and talked over them. You can record your voice by plugging a microphone into your computer, and you can fill it with video recordings to make a great video clip. This is enough to make a good product called a digital product.

In addition to paper books, I published an e-book under a different pen name in Korea. The book has been sold on Korean e-book sites as a best seller, and it continues to be on the top of the list for over a year now. The advantage of e-books is that they generate a high rate of royalties to authors. E-books can save money in production and distribution costs, so the author makes a minimum profit of 50 to 90 percent. Authors of paper books, on the other hand, receive 10 percent royalties.

That's why e-books may be cheaper and shorter than paper books, allowing you as an author to concentrate only on the topic you want to cover. Because the price is low, and even if the book is sold at a small rate, it provides a high rate of return to the author. I have published 11 English e-books on Amazon with my wife. I wrote a short e-book about meditation, which people also buy as a paper book version on Amazon.

Butterfly Investment generated revenue even before the company was founded, by sending out documents about business ideas that are based on the concept of zero-base startup. It's an intangible document—a digital—but it's filled with the business models and spirit of starting a business without any capital. Through this document, I continue to discover new items and develop new business lines as I conduct sales training. There continues to be a growing number of entrepreneurs who sell special products at a minimum cost using the zero-base startup method.

Butterfly Investment is using PDF documents as an official product that produces tangible results by selling intangible products. While some of the offline supplements have been added over time, I maintain a firm foundation for intangible services so that people can use our services anywhere in the world.

More and more entrepreneurs from Butterfly Investment membership are turning up with Amazon e-book publications. In addition to overseas e-book releases, this continues to challenge me to produce video lectures so that I can sell them overseas.

There are some concerns about intangible products. An intangible product is likely to cost less and be borrowed against frequently when one starts a business without a physical company office. Therefore, people might think that only digital products can be used for a zero-base startup. In fact, any type of product—digital or physical—can be used in a zero-base startup business. Still, I want to make this clear here that intangible products, or digital products, exist in the world in various ways and many people aren't yet familiar with.

There are some people who are more likely familiar with offline businesses and physical products than others who are more familiar with online businesses. People who don't know about the existence of digital products but are accustomed to online business may soon give up if they pursue offline business only.

Also, if you neglect offline business because you realize you can sell digital products, you can use only half of the market. There are certain areas where synergy occurs when you use online and offline together. There's a reason I prefer to be online but still stayed offline for five years, conducting regular lectures and forums. This is because there's a field of energy that occurs when people meet offline, which online cannot replace.

When I was struggling before I started my own business, I continuously read the classics about the wealthy people. I was inspired during those difficult times, but there are also things that helped me over time. Real rich people can feel like money floats in the air. Thus, I believe that if you put your mind to it, you can "convert anything into money." Plus, I never forget the common knowledge that real rich people live happily away from competition and zero-sum games, and I wanted to live that way. Just as they think money floats in the air, they believe that intangible products can be worth a lot of money. I was working to make this possible in Butterfly Investment, and we have created quite a few examples. I also wanted to push the limit of the Republic of Korea, so I learned from people who make money abroad.

It may take time, but I will never stop formalizing that approach and helping CEOs of zero-base startups to sell more products. One of the things I'm really glad about is this: If I gave up and collapsed in the middle of the day, who else would have tried this project?

I'm proud to be one of the few people to build up my own unique case of zero-base startups from the beginning and to cultivate a way to sell intangible products. I've seen senior executives and small business executives mostly stick to physical products, and I tell these stories during my lecture to get rid of the limitations of a product line. If so far you've only been interested in selling physical products, please take a bold look at intangible and digital products. There will be a new world that makes money from the air.

12. The Fourth Industrial Revolution: Salespreneurship is a must-have.

The Fourth Industrial Revolution is the issue these days. During the Third Industrial Revolution, which was a transition from analogue to digital in the 1980s, at one point or another the Fourth Industrial Revolution came into our lives. We can see the technological innovation in the fields of artificial intelligence, big data analysis, robotics, unmanned transport, and the Internet of Things (IoT) which will lead to the Fourth Industrial Revolution. Therefore, articles related to these areas are often published. The Presidential Fourth Industrial Revolution Committee has been established, so events and news related to this will continue for quite a while. As people look at the news, they wonder if we should learn coding now to prepare for the Fourth Industrial Revolution. Otherwise, people might consider, if they had to abandon their majors, what new major would they choose for the Fourth Industrial Revolution and how to seize the opportunity.

It might be a natural phenomenon that the media is drawing attention to. As it continues to cover the issue, we see increases in the number of businesses involved in the Fourth Industrial Revolution and an increase in support for startups in related fields. However, it would be difficult to seize a special opportunity if one were to respond to an issue abruptly. Opportunities must come first for those who have continued to study and perform in relevant fields diligently. Regardless of the issue, those who continue their favorite research can now expand their choices and capacity.

About 10 years ago in Korea, there was a soy chicken restaurant craze. Everybody started a chicken restaurant. Every day a new brand was born. However, the boom suddenly burst, and the trendy chicken shops went belly up. Similarly, franchises such as small beer bars also became popular two to three years ago in Korea. As a result, new brands and stores were popping up every day. The boom went without a hitch, and then many shops collapsed within a year. If people jumped into fashion without any particular reason to choose this industry, they will surely pay the price. That's because the boom isn't entirely made up of itself. Recognizing that they're lucky to make money out of fashion, people can prepare and study to survive even if they're out of fashion.

If customers come in and sales revenue is high, but the owner just sits still, then the trend is over. Or if competition becomes fierce and the guests aren't coming, an owner might get to the point where they couldn't handle it. Only people who can see objectively whether or not they are making money from the trend can survive in the end. And such vision can be maintained when they're still at the point of sales and close to customers.

A quick entry into the Fourth Industrial Revolution may give you a chance to make money. However, it's necessary to be wary of becoming a founder who is not blinded by the flash of big money and loses their survival instinct in the long run.

There are certain advantages to entering the market first. But what's more important is that the company can hold out until it's branded with products or services that give trust to clients. Prior to Google's launch, there was a search engine called AltaVista. There was a personal computer even before Apple I. However, people remember Google as a major search engine and Apple I as the first personal computer. How quickly you enter the market doesn't determine how long you'll survive in the market. The boom in the Fourth Industrial Revolution will create many businesses, and many others will disappear. In the future, some people's jobs will be replaced by robots and artificial intelligence. The change is constantly being created, and if we don't prepare for the Fourth Industrial Revolution now, it feels like we might be in some big trouble sooner or later.

But think about it. The pace at which the world is changing is getting faster. These innovations may come again in the near future. What would it be like to live by reacting to the situation and repeating being trendy each time? In Korea, educational policies change whenever the administration is changed. Accordingly, math aptitude test preparation tools for students will change and might bring quite a lot of confusion to students. Regardless of the SAT (a standardized scholastic aptitude test used for college admission), students who like and enjoy studying are less likely to suffer from these changes. When policy changes, only those students who change their study direction according to the job outlook and change their career paths according to their parents' concerns continue to wander and stress.

Years ago, a TOEIC (Test of English for International Communication in Korea) score was required to prepare for the exam to become a government officer, and I got the score I wanted right after taking the test

However, I had never attended a TOEIC academy. I thought it was natural to get good grades when I practiced reading and listening accordingly.

When I was going to take a test, there was a time when the TOEIC format changed, and they named it the new TOEIC. If I studied for the TOEIC mechanically, practicing tips, then it would be a quite a problem. In fact, there were many people who had a difficult time because their scores dropped significantly on the new TOEIC format. However, I didn't feel much about the changes since I was used to the old format, and I got the grade I wanted without any problem.

What I'm emphasizing through salespreneurship is the essence of business. When starting a business, it's essential to listen to the inner voice of the founder, not the outer voice. It's bound to take time. However, the only thing that can save time is getting close to sales.

Sales experience can develop an inner voice for the founder. An inner voice doesn't respond to the chaotic changes from outside. Sales experience is required to enable the founder to recover quickly from failure.

Some inner voices are made from an illusion of outer voices. Recognizing such cases can also be put to use at the contact point with the customer during the sale. Sales experience helps one distinguish fake voices and focus on the real ones.

I also had time to think while reading a book and news related to the Fourth Industrial Revolution. But I didn't waver. Watching someone make an innovation, I focus on how to use it. Rather than trying to enter the market that is now trendy and in fashion, I am just going to use the results of people making innovation in our business. For instance, someone continues to create tools to help sell with big data analytics and artificial intelligence. In particular, such tools are being developed overseas. By providing such information to my business, I can increase sales and prepare for overseas expansion.

The Fourth Industrial Revolution has only been around for a few years, but it's become a difficult force to ignore. However, your mind is the essence of your business, and the first thing you care about is what you're talking about and what you're selling. If the essence remains stable, the company can enjoy full benefits whenever the fifth and sixth industrial revolutions take place. That would be one of the key benefits for the founder who focuses on salespreneurship.

13. It's a great illusion that the value increases only if it's added.

There's a reason YG Entertainment, one of the biggest production companies in Korea for famous Korean singers and boy/girl groups, is good at promoting its singers. YG Entertainment even makes a video of singers being selected as members for its training course, and then shows it on TV. The singers begin their debut after already securing a large fan base, showing the progress from a normal student who is constantly scolded to an idol. Then, even if someone starts out as a group band with similar members, the public will single out the individual performer. That's how to add value to the story, and it doesn't have to be a success story. When frustration and despair and joy and success are combined, the story itself reveals its greatest value. In fact, it's something to add to the value chain.

Let's move on to the next story. What determines the price when we buy a computer or a camera? Hardware quality and cost are considered. Depending on how expensive the CPU is and how expensive the lenses are, the price of electronics varies. The more you add, the higher the value, the higher the price seems to be the truth. Even if you're given a message, the cost increases with the time added as you generally feel it's worth adding more time. It's a very natural story, and it's based on common sense.

We can take the case of someone selling samgyetang (Korean version of chicken soup with ginseng). Regular samgyetang is sold at 11,000 won, while mung bean samgyetang (red bean soup) and Western chicken soup are sold at 15,000 won. Why is that? I think they're more valuable because they contain more expensive ingredients, so people are willing to pay higher prices. After that, people begin to feel confident that the only way to get higher prices is to add value. And I think all of the products and services that are priced around the world fit into this formula.

From these examples, there may be no doubt that a higher value is needed to get a higher price. You may have felt this while reading this book; however, I don't like stories without dissent. In this regard, I would like to share in this chapter a story that can be divided in the way that values are given. There are many ways that a startup can consider to add value to products and services. My favorite way is to add value from accumulated stories and content from the founder.

The service is similar to the service provided by rivals, and it's a shining example when the content is different. Moreover, it takes a long time to build up the story. Therefore, not only the people who already started businesses stress this but also the people who are ready to start one. That's because it's difficult to share the accumulated story unless it's recorded, even if the founder thinks there might not be much to show during the preparation period. Nonetheless, it's necessary to include the preparation process to be recorded for starting a business, and every story should become a valuable story to be shared in the process of success.

Now, I would like to talk about a strange pricing formula. People in Germany drink a lot of beer. When people visit Germany, they drink beer instead of water. This is because beer is delicious, but also because its price is similar to or cheaper than water's. The Czech Republic, next to Germany, is also known as a destination where beer is cheaper than water.

If you think about it, beer is made of water and something is added to it, but it's not generally understood that it's cheaper than water. Simply adding doesn't create value. There are some things that vary depending on what kind of water or beer it is, but we have to admit to people's response to the fact that there's no price reflection, even though something's added.

Years ago, IRIVER and Yepp took the MP3 market first with their hardware and technology, but Apple later dominated it with its iPod. When the hardware-driven company received high prices for adding extra technology to its MP3 player, Apple only focused on making it easier to listen to high-quality music. In the end, Apple made iTunes software, not hardware, for their clients.

It was not like the other two companies that made hardware more expensive, giving it value, and receiving higher prices. By cutting out all unnecessary steps to the experience of listening to music, Apple also saved money by developing more technologies. Then, it got a vote from customers as a more valuable product.

Now you'll start to get a sense of what it's like to get more valuable by taking a little off.

Choi used to run math academies for students in Korea. The institute also made its own textbooks, Then, later, he established a publishing company to exclusively publish and distribute the math textbooks that he made. Choi created and published about 50 math books within a year. It seems like a huge volume. But if you look at the full number of math problems included in the 50 textbooks, they're similar to what's in one math book or two, and the price per book is about the same. In other words, Choi's books are about 50 times more expensive. Some people may be tilting their heads from this point on.

"Who buys such a book?"

Of course, most parents don't buy the book. People who make decisions on quantity and price alone will not even look at this book, especially if they read it. Then, why did he made the books this way? I'll explain the background of this book. Anyone who has ever solved a long list of math problems will know. How long does it take to go over just one page? The typical old math workbook is about studying only the front pages, but not moving forward.

Why is that? It's because it's packed with as many problems as possible to make parents, not students, happy. Therefore, it's difficult to solve problems without a notebook, and it's easy to get bored immediately because there are no pictures. Not even a single sheet can be given away. Naturally, the idea that mathematics is a boring subject dominates to the children.

Choi, who had a son in school, started making fast page-turning books for his son. There are one or two problems on a page, a picture, and a lot of blank space in his books. A child can finish one book in just one day if he wants to. In this format, only one or two existing math books can turn into 50 books. Of course, nine out of 10 parents tell their children to use the old economical math books and solve them. Most parents focus on the cost per problem.

However, there are some parents who see their children getting tired of math and feel the seriousness of losing interest in math. They hope their children will love math for life, or at least longer while they're still in school. I think it's better to spend money wisely not to be a math quitter until the college SAT, which will eventually save money. Parents who agree on this philosophy buy about 50 books in a package for their children.

There are only a few, if any, customers who applaud subtraction and value it. We added value to The Coffee Club by excluding information or specifications about clients when setting up blind dates. Harulab (http://harulab.kr/) is helping people write a book in one day, and it's adding value by helping people shorten the time it takes them to write a book. It's a stereotype that it has to cost more if it takes longer.

Let's say it costs $100,000 for one month to do an important project. But what would it be worth if you could solve such projects elsewhere in only a week? Since you've done less work, is it correct to give less money? Or is it better to give more money since you've finished the time-consuming task quickly?

I think the latter is true. Why do people want to come to Butterfly Investment at the expense of high consulting costs? They come because they can fix things they'll be thinking about for a year or five years by themselves; however, I'm helping them to solve problems in a short period of time.

Is it worth helping to solve problems over a long period of time? Is it worth helping to fix them in a short time? There's a justification for taking more money, not because it requires more time, but because it requires less time.

There's a stereotype among people that a negative is a devaluation, and a positive is adding value. For those who still naturally believe this stereotype, let me give one last example. What does minus mean in mathematics? For instance, what is the answer to 1 - (- 1)? It is 2. We do the subtraction, but the number becomes bigger. If you only think that adding something is only adding the value, you're out of touch with a sophisticated business model, creating only rising costs, putting in more effort, more hassle, and more communication problems.

Butterfly Investment is focused on pulling back and making things simple by subtracting unnecessary things. In particular, it's about subtracting the negatives. There must be something positive about someone who is considered negative. Most people think it's a plus to release the specifications in dating services. However, some people think it's a minus to release the information. When you take out the negative parts of such a service, you increase the value, and you approach clients with special values. Many other examples can be found that can also demonstrate these concepts.

In my book, I mention expensive services and value giving. However, I could have limited myself to raising the price by adding additional services. So, as I mentioned above, I just want you to put aside the stereotype that only adding makes value.

If you like this book, please leave your honest review on Amazon.

These reviews really help me as an author to get my book in front of more people just like you. Thank you!

Chapter 2. Salespreneurship-Mind

1.The limit of the word "sales."

There was no spoken language in primitive times. People communicated only with facial expressions and voice pitch. But one of them had the ability to speak and was treated as a wizard because the word from the wizard's mouth became a thing in the real world.

In particular, in ancient Japan, words like "words" and "what happens in real life" were used interchangeably with the word *goto* (☒☒). This story tells us the power of speech and the power of language. Many proverbs tell the power of a word. Every word counts. There is a Korean saying, "A horse without legs runs down the street," which means that words or rumors spread rapidly. It's obvious that people have always been interested in the value of words and language and their power to spread.

The word *kotodama*, which refers to the Japanese word "soul of language" and "spirit of language" expresses the power of a word. Words also have souls. So you must be careful about saying negative things. Gossip is said to be the fastest way to ruin the person who talks behind the scenes.

I've studied language and its effects on people. I studied hypnotism and know that language has a strong influence on the unconscious, so I tend to pay a great deal attention to the use of language. I happened to come across the *Book of Changes* (a Chinese classic on divination) while I was doing a variety of related studies.

I thought the *Book of Changes* was based on science, and that it was reasonable and rational. I went to a lecture on the idea that the book would help business, and I also read several books. There's a Korean saju cafe-fortunetelling house, which I go to from time to time, where there's a teacher who studied Chinese divination for a long time. I talk with my teacher there from time to time.

I once had the following conversation with the teacher.

"Master [teacher], what if I study the *Book of Changes* properly?"

"It's no bad thing studying the *Book of Changes*," he replied.

Being embarrassed by asking the obvious questions, I asked again. "May I ask what's the best wisdom you've gained from studying the *Book of Changes*?"

The teacher said briefly, pondering, "Be careful of what I am saying."

I've read various self-help books that mention the power of words and language. Religious books also have many stories that tell the greatness of words. I found again that the *Book of Changes* considers the power of words to be important.

There's a reason for this rambling talk about the power of speech. Recall the word "sales " or "selling" now and recall the images and feelings that are associated with these words. What kind of feeling comes out of the word "sales"? Is it negative? Or is it positive? Is it pleasant or unpleasant? I guess it's more like a negative feeling. How can I say this? It's been a long time since I've felt in the field how people experience the word "sales" and its associated words.

Few people welcomes a salesperson that is visiting. Few people like to be assigned to the sales department. Few people openly claim to be a good salesperson. Growing the business, the project team is important; personnel management is also important. Marketing is also key, and the finance team is also significant. But there is one very important element in developing the business. It is the sales. Sales revenue can facilitate other departments to work, and so other elements can help grow sales revenue and grow the business.

So why did "sales" get such a bad and cruel image? With the word "sales," some salesperson has pushed for it, forced their friends and families to buy the products, made it difficult for friends to understand their behavior, and as a result, destroyed relationships.

Although I have worked as a salesperson for a long time, I know it's much more important for a company to increase its performance immediately than for employees to keep their old relationships. Even if the valuable relationship between sales representatives is cut off, the company encourages them to sell the products right away. It's also comforting to know that this can be an opportunity to reorganize unwanted connections.

What do you think? For this reason, the word "sales" doesn't receive the spotlight and treatment it deserves. The word "sales," which has generated people's negative feelings because of the wrong sales approach, is still being rejected. Sales are still considered a chore and a lower-class task.

I wrote this book with concrete determination. I want to release the resentment of the word "sales." Only then can readers of this book become familiar with sales, sell their products, and earn the money they want from their businesses. Otherwise, whenever you recall the words "sales" along with the concept of "being forced to buy the products," negative memories from the past will arise.

Now it's time to see the word "sales" through a new lens.

If you don't go through this process, your mind will pause every time you try to sell something for your business. The better you perform this process of changing the perception of the word, the less resistance you have to sales, and this leads to higher sales revenue. Eventually, it leads to a successful independent business startup with no capital in advance.

There is a psychological technique called NLP (neuro-linguistic programming) that helps convert the way we think. Simply put, it's a technique to observe the automatic neural responses familiar with the past, and to come up with new and better ways to respond.

People who have suffered from trauma can realize beneficial effects by observing their trauma using NLP techniques to reframe their experiences.

The same can be applied to change the negative images you get from hearing the word "sales." I've changed such negative thoughts, and all the people I've been coaching to produce explosive sales results are equipped with new ways of thinking. When you think of "sales," you should create a new pathway in your way of thinking and your neural network so that the idea of sales becomes acceptable. It's necessary to first admit that the image of "sales"— being pushed, stressed, or damaged—has a bad association that was thoroughly taken from the outside. Afterward, you must reinterpret the word "sales" into a positive image and make it easier to accept. For those of you who have admitted to having a bad association with the word in the past, I propose the following reinterpretation of "sales."

The businessperson is the one who solves the customers' annoying and bothering problems. But you have the tools to solve the customers' problems well and provide them. This is the "sales" that deliver the tool to customers and makes them happy and willing to pay.

Sales are an inevitable and integral part of solving customer problems. Take Butterfly Investment, for instance. The potential clients of Butterfly Investment are the ones who unconditionally think that starting a business requires money and capital and that they should receive investments and loans in advance. They'll soon have problems with starting a business with a lot of money when they aren't ready to sell their products yet. And there's fear of losing money. Or the ones who have already failed a great deal in business by relying on a large amount of investment that didn't lead to selling the products are potential customers of Butterfly Investment. To solve their problems, Butterfly Investment offers free materials and videos that give inspiration to independent startups with no capital.

These materials are going to help solve the problems in their businesses. But for those who can't solve the problems alone, who would rather be motivated to join the community and read more materials and watch more videos that can be disclosed for free, there's also a paid service within Butterfly Investment.

A paid service is used as a tool for those who want to use time and money and engage in positive and refined exchanges. Abroad, there are also customers using these services from Butterfly Investment. I'm proud to say that I've made good tools to solve entrepreneurs' problems and am selling my tools with pride at least a few times for the price they paid.

With that in mind, I don't have any loopholes flowing from the negative ideas about sales. I never put any pressure on my customers to buy my products. There's no reason not to be proud of selling my products. If you don't know what's wrong with the customer in their life and only talk about the good points of the product you want to sell, you'll never be able to sell it properly. And it only makes the negative perception of sales stronger for you and your customers.

Be sure to achieve a reframing on sales. "Sales" is not selling products. It's a process meant to solve customers' problems. You get paid because it solves the problems well. And the tools that will solve the problem are the services or products you've created. We'll cover these areas in more detail in later chapters.

Changing the entrepreneur's thinking has a great impact on business. If you have to make important choices in business and take action, but you stay in the mindset of the past, it will make you lose your energy. Then this mindset won't help speed up projects, but instead you will be dragging them for a long time.

You'll feel it in business. The obstacles are not all in sight. Hidden barriers are often much higher. My new approach to business is optimized to clear away invisible barriers. One of the approaches I talk about is the entrepreneur's reframing the word "sales." Of course, this approach can ensure good performance not only for the entrepreneurs but also for the sales representatives of any company. I hope that you can apply this approach to your products and services to release the brakes and speed up the sales.

2. Why you can't take the lead in your sales.

If you were active in preparing to start a business, you would have collected a variety of information for a sales method.

It's likely that you might memorize details about the product, from its benefits to its disadvantages over the competition.

Perhaps this isn't enough, and you may also have an invincible line of comments to respond to any rejection from your customers. It's at least a basic preparation that you are ready to sell and to be familiar with this content when meeting with a customer.

However, people become so attached to what they prepared that they might lose the lead in sales after all. You might be confused by what I said just now. It's natural to be confused. To turn the current question mark into an exclamation mark before this chapter is finished, it's necessary to answer the following questions first.

Is the person who takes the lead in the conversation a big talker? Or are they the one who makes less? You might want to think about the sales figures you see around you. Were the salespeople talking a lot? Or was it the other way round?

I guess it was the salespeople who were mainly talking a lot. It's most likely that readers have considered the person who talks a lot to be the leader of the conversation. Our perception is that people who are high in the hierarchy often take hold of the microphone, talk a lot, and lead the overall conversation.

When a company holds a meeting, many of its seniors talk while juniors listen, and many of the juniors naturally follow the decisions made based on what the leaders said. However, this is more like a notification rather than the desired outcome of a conversation. However, "sales"—or the selling process—is different from this one-way conversation.

The process in which goods are delivered with the exchange of payment between customers and sales associates is the sum of time during which emotional exchanges between clients and sales associates occur, as well as the stories through which they are exchanged. In this process, if a salesperson wants to talk more to get the upper hand in order to sell products more, he or she is very misguided.

In fact, it's a person with few words who really takes the lead in a conversation. The dominant player in this conversation is the listener, not the talker. Of course, it's not enough to just listen, and the person in the position to ask the relevant questions properly and listen to the answers carefully can take the lead. Why is that? By listening to the other person's story by asking questions, you'll know more about the other person's needs. Moreover, if you listen to the other person's story, the other person will try to tell you more stories about himself or herself. That way, you'll be able to hear even deeper information about them.

Does the person leading the conversation know a lot more about the topic or less? Having learned more about the topic while asking the questions you need answers with, you'll have the opportunity to guide the direction of the conversation and to make favorable decisions throughout the conversation.

Although we've had a few moments to think about it, many of the sales scenes around us are having conversations in a structure that will never proceed to sales. The customer keeps asking questions, and the salesperson keeps talking about the products.

Sometimes, when sensitive questions are asked, some salespeople respond emotionally. How can a salesperson who just keeps answering questions and shows emotional disorganization take the lead in a conversation? And can they produce the results of selling the products? It will never work that way.

Ways to improve sales performance are described throughout this book. This part makes a point to ensure that the salesperson takes the lead in the conversation.

The first is, as I said, you have to be in the position of asking questions, not just explaining the products. However, this isn't easy and requires much effort because the salesperson would like to tell the customer about the products and services more and more as soon as the customer asks a question. And it's hard to break this pattern once the salesperson starts to talk, as there are so many things the salesperson has prepared and even memorized to say in front of the customer.

In particular, there are many people who can't stand silence and are nervous about being silenced even for a few seconds during a conversation. And it's difficult to stay still if the customer feels uncomfortable during that static period.

Because of these factors, it's difficult for a salesperson to keep his or her mouth shut. However, you must stick to the listening position. Otherwise, you won't be able to hear the customer.

Only when you listen to the client can you customize the sales points. A few salespeople seem to be so insincere as to memorize popular comments and pass the benefits to clients. Even if you're selling, you have to give examples and explanations that fit their position and problems to help the customer better understand the product.

The same goes for lectures. I ask the whole class what they do and what they're interested in doing when they come in small classes. I talk about different stories to college students, cases suitable for self-employed business owners, and stories suitable for office workers. Naturally, understanding of the lecture can only be improved.

The second point for the salesperson is that the product must not be placed between the customer and the salesperson. The product descriptions shouldn't be the main topic of the conversation. On the general sales scene, salespeople meet with the customer, and make "ceremonial ice breaking." Then they present memorized benefits of the product and the keywords associated with the product.

For instance, you have a formal conversation with a potential client and immediately talk about the person being a new employee, and then you suddenly start talking about the new insurance product right away. You make this mistake if the product is on your mind, and you put it on the table anytime you want. Goods must not be placed on the negotiating table with the customer.

Asking questions and listening to customers should lead them to the inconveniences and problems they want to solve naturally. And you should raise such issues as topics of conversation. The salesperson must ask the customer relevant questions with a view to proactively resolve them. Customers will also be more willing to engage in dialogue to find a solution to a problem when it's a true pain they would like to resolve in their life.

Rather than listening to talk about a new product, they find it more comfortable to talk about themselves.

Then, there is a third consideration. Simply asking a profound question might not be enough. You should listen to the customer's answer carefully. You should nod and respond to what the customer said. Of course, it's much more effective if you have a genuine reaction.

Let's think for a moment. How many people are around you who genuinely sympathize with you and listen to your problems? There aren't many. Most people mainly want to tell their own stories. It's very difficult to find people who empathize and listen to someone else's stories. So when you ask questions and sympathize with the customer, they can comfortably share much more information about themselves.

While sufficient information is available about the problem, the salesperson associates the way to solve the problem with his product. Or they can lead the conversation by looking for problems that can be solved with products. You can include subtle nuances like that if you think your product will fix the customer's problem enough.

In the previous chapter, "The limit of the word "sales.", the salesman told the customer that he was a problem fixer, not a seller. And the product is just a tool to help. That way, the salesperson can confidently talk about his product, which is a good solution to the customer's problem. But let me show you how to speak more skillfully.

There's a way to lead a conversation by asking questions early and communicating about customer issues. Otherwise, no effect will be produced. The way is not to talk about your product until the customer first asks you to fix the problem.

If you keep this in mind when you ask questions and lead the conversation, the customer will naturally inquire about the solution to the problem. When you lead the conversation this way, the customer will naturally ask about the products first, and then you can give them a description of the product while giving customized examples and stories. You aren't talking about the product first, but making the customer realize what they need.

In such situations, you can talk about products more proudly and have fewer objections to selling them. It's likely to feel that you're consulting with your clients for free, and they'll feel the same way.

A phenomenon is created when a salesperson takes the lead in a conversation. Of course, the ratio of actual selling is much higher, and the customer satisfaction ratio is higher than that of customers who paid after listening to unilateral explanations from the seller. What you memorized and prepared to take the lead in the conversation may have been blocking the conversation's lead.

Please remember the points covered in this chapter. The real sales masters who listen to their clients genuinely, customize, and easily sell won't tell you about their know-how easily. Or they don't even realize what they're doing.

3. Without exception, sales always come first.

Everyone talks about the importance of sales in business. However, it's difficult to be told that you should sell before everything else. As it's a difficult story to listen to, I've made it easier to hear in this book. Nothing is put in front of the sale if there's a bid to start a new business as a zero-base startup. Sales are a top priority for zero-base startups. Let's take a moment to explore why sales should be a priority compared to other startup processes.

First, sales come before writing a business proposal or a business plan. You need to develop your sales capacity as well as build up know-how to sell your products first before you get investment from outside.

Business plans must be established when you start a business. The above proposal or plan refers to a business plan to receive investment specifically. The business plan to receive the investment from venture capital or angel capital is a painstaking plan. I saw the people who were preparing it, and it was almost enough to produce a book. It's imperative that the business plan should appeal to investors as undervalued. That's because you should include the plausible plans to get more investments. Once you successfully win big investments, you get a little higher value and a little more recognition from the public. However, if you get investors and sign contracts based on such a project plan, what you wrote in the project plan could hold you back later.

If the steps of the plan aren't likely to be followed properly, the investor might take an excessive managerial intervention to protect the investment. The more investors are invested in a business plan without the founder's own sales results soon to follow, the more likely the investors will change and try to get involved in the business. If you start a type of business that can never be started without investment, it will become the business of the investors themselves rather than your own business.

Second, sales come before the survey.

There are entrepreneurs who would like to call around for market surveys before launching the product and company. Usually, they ask questions like these: "Do you think certain types of services or products are necessary for your daily life?" "Do you think it's expensive at this price?" When they're asked whether they'd like to recommend the product or service once it's released, most people will respond in favor of it.

Upon receiving the survey results, the founder is excited about the positive responses. And they think they won't take a back seat when their services are introduced to the world. However, it's hard to expect the same level of customer response or reaction as seen in the initial survey when they launched the service or started selling products.

Why is that? It's a fake survey. It's a fake survey because the founder believed the customer would really pay for the product or service as they said yes to the survey. If you want to know what the real customer thinks, you should tell them to pay for it right away. Or tell them to put down their deposit.

"Do you have any intention to buy the product later?"

"Yes," they answer without any thought.

"Thank you," you reply and think, *Oh, I got one customer. Yes!*

It's unfortunate, but it's only a moratorium on rejection. Sales, not just surveys, can be rejected immediately, and expectations can be avoided. And you can hear the real reason why the real customer refused to buy.

"Do you have any intention to buy the product later?"

"Yes," they answer without any thought.

"Thank you. Then why don't you put down your deposit now?"

Then, feeling surprised, the customer says what they really think. "Oh, yeah, but … it's more expensive than I thought."

Is it a good idea to listen to the customer's real inner thoughts later? Or do you think we should hear them as soon as possible? Of course, you should listen as soon as possible. You can't hear the real story of a customer without actually selling. Don't delay your refusal any longer. Don't swear at a prospective customer as later they turn down your product. It's the fault of the founder who didn't actually try to sell it and didn't listen to the real story from the customer.

Third, sales come before making a fancy web page. Nowadays, it's regarded as strange if there's no homepage for startups. However, it's better not to create a homepage if it's not managed properly or updated regularly. If you outsource to make a good web page, it can cost at least a few hundred to a few thousand dollars, and it would require a huge budget at the beginning of your business. It's also better to delay making web pages until after you've tried to sell as many products as possible. Moreover, with the money you earn from the sales, you can build your own homepage later.

Even before the website is created, there are many online channels to let consumers know about the product. You can also use blogs, and explain products directly through social networks such as Instagram, Facebook, and Pinterest. Otherwise, you can attract customers and promote by holding a business presentation offline.

As you go through this process, you should post the refined product introduction on your homepage. As a result, it's better to have an improved and sophisticated website by adjusting prices, aligning customer feedback, and deleting unnecessary items, all of which are based on experience from actual sales. If the company continues to post the corrections on its homepage, it will cause confusion among its customers. When selling to a small number of customers offline, it's manageable even if there's some confusion. Creating a homepage can also be more effective if it's done after enough sales are generated, to reduce disruption to clients.

Fourth, sales come before manufacturing.

It costs money to make things in advance. Entrepreneurs from zero-base startups earn the money they need from sales and then manufacture the products from that money. An example of a company that started this way is ISUIT, which sells customized suits and provides personal style consulting services. After hearing explanations about the suit design and consulting services offered to the customer by ISUIT, the manufacturer makes the suit through a partnership with the customer with the money the customer pays in advance.

A similar business model is used for DOEDGETTON, which provides wallet consulting. Normally, manufacturing and selling a wallet would require a wallet designer, materials, and a factory. However, the company has come up with a plan to sell its wallet, to provide a guide to become friends with money just like rich people and to give guidance on how the rich can use their wallet. They spend money on production later. A manufacturing business can also receive payment from customers in advance for their production costs, and maintain their business at their margins.

Fifth, sales come before corporate establishment.

There's a registration cost involved to establish a company; however, entrepreneurs from zero-base startups don't set up a company first at their own expense. First, they sell the products and service, receive payment from the customers, and then save the money to establish a company. It doesn't cost that much to start a company. If a company doesn't need a physical office at first, the founder can use a virtual address service for offices, and they can use the Bium Co. tax service firm cofounded with Butterfly Investment, using associated tax accountants at a low cost.

If you want to use a virtual address service, you can get a good deal from the Doran Doran Center located in Gangnam Station. For those who want to use actual office space and also use an address, CityCube Center (a shared office space, http://citycube.co.kr/) will be the perfect option as it has several branches in each part of Seoul at reasonable prices.

It's too late to generate sales if the founder tries to give the company a decent office and establish all the administrative setups first. You can generate sales before you set up an actual company, and you can get an office space later with that money from the sales. Expenses incurred during the company founding process may also be recognized as business-related costs after the company is established.

To people who come to Butterfly Investment and try to start a zero-base startup, I continue to give this message: "Get on with the sales process first." Naturally, it's cumbersome. They have some hard times at first as it's an unfamiliar process; nevertheless, they eventually sell their products and services first and start to set up their own company. I see this as a minimum requirement for entrepreneurs. If only founders start this way can they become more capable of selling their products and lasts longer. Even if they fail as a company, they'll still be able to make money and be able to make a comeback.

Even if the company goes bankrupt, the founders can still start over. All those sales experiences were built up and can be reflected in the next business and the chances of success are raised for the next one. All this is possible because the founder tried to sell the products first. Remember, sales come first without exception.

4. Ask forgiveness, not permission.

"Ask forgiveness, not permission."

That's an expression commonly used to describe the venture spirit and entrepreneurship. Literally, it means to ask for forgiveness rather than to ask for permission. The expression has some parts that are difficult to understand intuitively, so I'll talk about them now.

When it comes to business development and starting a company, there are some entrepreneurs who concern themselves too much about things in advance. In particular, legal and customer satisfaction areas tend to be considered as conservatively as possible. They believe that they must resolve more than 90 percent of these issues before they can start the company or launch products.

For instance, they'll seek counsel from several lawyers for possible legal conflicts and will push ahead with projects to find ways to divert such conflicts beforehand. The same happens in pursuit of the customers' satisfaction level. The business hasn't even started yet, but they are seeking permission to launch a service or product that is first customized to the most difficult customers from their imagination.

There is no 100 percent perfect service or product you will find if you start looking for a way to get completeness before you start your business. And once you start seeking perfection, you'll end up with your tail between your legs.

That's why many startups spend all their money preparing for the project before the launch. What I want to tell the founders of startups who are scared to launch, and who delay while seeking perfection, is this: "Ask for forgiveness rather than permission."

They should be discouraged by the mere requests for recurring permissions, which lower costs. If nothing goes ahead, they change their mind. They wonder if they should shut down the business, or go into business first, and then fix problems later. Why is that? Many of the issues covered before the launch aren't considered seriously in reality. Or, in the real world, it's easy to resolve the problems with a single comment or act.

If you break into your desk in advance to fix all problems before they start, you might lose your energy. Preparing an axe would be enough to solve the problems, but you're building a cannon for your potential problems. And when a problem occurs in real life, you're bound to come up with a better and simpler way to solve it from the field. It's difficult to think of creative solutions when you're under pressure to think about problems in advance and to solve them all perfectly.

Let's imagine that the founder thought it would be necessary to detect empty boxes from all the sealed packages. So as alternatives before they actually open the factory, the founder wonders, "Should we hire someone else who only finds empty boxes?" And then, "Can humans make mistakes, and should we use expensive X-ray equipment?"

But once a factory is opened and starts operating, the founder can think more realistically.

"Do I have to pay more for it than I already paid?"

The empty box feels light in the hands. The box containing the goods is heavy. It's the wind that makes the empty boxes fly, and the heavy ones stay the same. So you turn on a few electric fans to fix this problem simply. Quick, easy, and simple. And it's even cheap!

When the press says that business items with unusual models are doing well, some people say, "I also thought about that idea, but someone is doing well already." I don't blame those who say so, or criticize them. If they're using such words while feeling disappointed about losing the business item, I would tell them not to be disappointed.

Developing business items, collecting information to launch them, getting feedback from prospective clients, and using it to produce actual sales are all part of starting the business. If somebody said they started a business similar to the one you wanted to start, but they haven't gone far with it, you have no reason to be disappointed while watching other people's success. There are too many people who try to start a business and only try to get permission from others, but don't actually launch the products on the market.

Don't get me wrong. I don't mean to diminish the importance of the pre-business review process. However, many people waste too much energy on the preparation process and couldn't even start because of problems they might face in the market.

I think the tendency of Koreans to pursue perfection and to avoid failure is also a contributing factor in those cases. We have thought that perfection reduces failure. However, unnecessary energy consumption that's wasted on trying to be perfect is often critical. It's necessary to prevent yourself beforehand from fizzling out and running out of energy that's to be used in the actual market.

Even if there's a legal issue, if there are no business items that are capable of resolving existing problems or inconveniences, if you have a customer base that's benefiting, you're capable of pushing ahead with the project. If that's really the case, the customers will respond by making purchases. Customers who benefit will want you to expand your services. By including the voice of such clients in the business, you can affect politics and even get to the stage of revising the law.

In fact, when a service such as the Callbus (www.callbus.com) in Korea was launched, all legal issues were left unresolved. However, we started our business, we started making good responses for our clients, and we expanded our business by solving legal issues.

Have you ever heard of a person who sells the land of the moon? His story appeared in the *New York Times*. Dennis Hope is the founder. You can also buy the land of the moon through a company called Lunar Embassy. There's also a Korean branch. There are many packaged goods, but they're not as expensive as expected. It's about USD 25.00 to receive a monthly certificate and membership card worth one acre of lunar property.

About six million people bought the moon's land from Lunar Embassy.

Unaware of this background, a person who hears about the business item might think about the legal issues first. Dennis Hope has actually sold the moon, taking ownership of it to the United States, Russia, and even the United Nations. It's a business that can never be carried out in the way in which a real estate business is usually ran. Some customers may have bought this service just for fun. Some customers may later have bought seriously to assert ownership of the moon when human beings actually live on the moon. However, those who view the project as just odd won't make purchases. Now, when six million people around the world are purchasing the land of the moon, it's become strange to say it's just a silly business.

People who have experienced problems should be refunded, and those who haven't purchased the product shouldn't be bothered. The founder started to make sales first with absurd projects, and then grew the business with a sophisticated attitude to seek forgiveness and recognition.

There are also many other examples of people launching projects that don't make sense and turning them into businesses that make sense when they've gathered fans and customers. Butterfly Investment is another example of promoting the idea of non-capitalized startups and running a venture capital company without capital.

Everyone wondered how a corporation could be formed and invested in without capital. It was treated like a strange company. Now, as the number of people who are established through the business without any capital increases, the number of people who recognize Butterfly Investment's business model increases exponentially with the number of companies known to it.

In the case of a National Assembly act that became an issue in 2017 in Korea, a measure was taken to delay it due to the objection of several small business people. If Korea Certification is made during customs clearance, the costs of certification are reflected in the increase in the price of goods. And it can't be a quick update of a product since it takes time to authenticate.

As for the bill, public hearings were omitted, and the bill was put into law. Small business owners figured out that the damage could be extensive. I don't mean to offend the law. Laws may also exist that go against the benefits of the person in charge and those involved. So they have the potential to revise the law at any time if it's justifiable.

If you're stuck in such laws and are unable to move your business, they're a load off your mind. But if you're confident in your business, and believe that it will solve larger social problems and have bigger benefits, you need to push back. So if your business makes the law change or affects the political world, you won't have to worry about the cost of marketing.

I think it's a gift given to the founder who has the attitude of asking forgiveness first without asking for permission. If you're just relaxing in the process of asking for permission, start with the opportunity to meet this book. The gift will come back anyway.

5. If you want to make the perfect product, start selling it when it isn't.

When you start your own business, you don't know what to prepare first. So you look around to see what other business owners are doing, and you follow what they're doing. Usually, people start up a new company with team building. And they make a team with friends from school, former coworkers, meeting partners, or family members.

After that, a founder usually develops business plans, takes chances on pitching for potential investors, and prepares presentations. Or they want to take out a loan from a bank to finance the initial project. Almost anyone who's trying to start a business starts in a similar way only after they've found enough capital and people power. They think it's necessary to take all of these steps to make the product perfect before they launch it in the market.

But there's something that the founders easily miss out on. They believe that only the perfect product from the start can be sold in the market. But this is just an illusion of starters. This chapter looks at why such an illusion is created and what approaches can be applied when they realize that it's an illusion.

One of the things commonly talked about in the training programs for startups is the *buyer's persona*. Simply put, it predicts in advance which customers will buy the company's services and products. It's designed to develop sales strategies and customer-friendly marketing methods based on the specific characteristics of the target customers.

So you study the gender, age, family members, job, financial situation, education level, residence, and so on of the potential customers to find out more about the people who will be the clients of the company. For instance, if you run a Facebook ad, you can set up a target customer based on these factors.

I'm also aware of the importance of the buyer's persona. In particular, since entrepreneurs with no capital are starting to focus on narrow targets in the non-mainstream market, they must identify the factors that may appeal to their target customers. At this stage, however, entrepreneurs naturally make the mistake of missing an important customer group.

What do they miss? And why? As we predict the details of a customer's information, at some point, the founder's head is occupied with a particular person and prepares the project according to the characteristics of that person. However, the more you make predictions about the person and get too much absorbed in that situation, the closer you get to the image of the most difficult and picky customer.

The more you perform customer analysis before sales, the more you become obsessed with creating perfect products to satisfy extremely demanding customers. You start to believe that it's an important mission for entrepreneurs even if it takes longer and more money. But if we start to portray these customers in the beginning phase of the business, it's bound to make business slow to progress and initial sales difficult. An extremely picky customer is one who can only be satisfied with the product over time as it becomes more complete. And one day, an important group of clients must be satisfied in the later stage of the business.

But if you focus on this group from the beginning of your business, you lose other important groups of customers. These clients are the ones who buy the product as they need them, even if it has a few flaws at first.

There are some customers who never pay for products that don't meet their own standards; however, there are many people who do. It's hard to believe, but it's true. Some customers are very picky, and they are standing out from the group, but there are so many other customers who aren't. So, what kind of people are paying for the product, regardless of the product's completeness? First, there are people who are familiar with or have trust in the business.

Or, they are the ones who need such a product or service badly but simply don't use it because they can't find a company that offers what they really need. Such people are ready to pay money if they find the product—even if it's a little less than perfect in the beginning—because it's sufficient to solve their problems well. Or they're curious and willing to test and pay for new products when they come out.

Early purchases lead to good relationships with the company, and whoever wants to be in the business later pays for them if they aren't significantly less perfect. The spectrum of clients who trust and buy services and products that have not yet been perfected is broader than expected.

"Sounds like you're asking me to find some pushovers?"

That's not the case at all. I'm not saying to cheat the customers by selling products. It's wrong to palm off what's lacking. However, it's important to keep those customers who are aware of the flaws in the beginning but are still willing to pay for the products.

For instance, a company may develop and sell products with five characteristics. If you try to sell after all five characteristics have been raised to the highest level, it takes a long time before revenue is generated. It also continues to cost money to complete all of the characteristics, adds to the company's communication costs, and misses the timing of product launch.

Then, when you actually try to sell the product, you might run out of cash and energy. Some customers feel pleased if they're satisfied with one or two characteristics they consider most important. They're not irrational, but rather are smart people.

They're very sure of their likes and dislikes when it comes to setting their values. Once you think about satisfying the most demanding customers with time and money until all the features of the product are made to the perfect level, the timing to begin selling is constantly off. Business moves away from success.

If you start selling products at 100 percent of the effort, 100 percent of the time and only 10 percent of your effort and time may affect sales, you'll waste unnecessary resources because you want to prepare thoroughly in advance. It's a good idea to prevent that.

Our story—that of one's startup of his own business through pre-sales—also has some aspects that are compatible with the MVP (minimum viable product), which is described in "Lean Startup Strategy." Starting with the minimum number of sales targets, the company will make sales first, receive feedback from customers, and continue to develop services. I'm talking about taking a step further and setting the minimum to zero to begin selling. Many of these cases and know-how related to this are specifically addressed in other chapters.

I hope there is no misunderstanding. I'm not saying to make perfect products. Of course, we must get to that stage of the business. Only then will the founder continue to gain the fame and profits he or she wants. But I wanted to show how inefficient and idealistic it is if the entrepreneur is planning to fully prepare the product and start selling it later.

A team and investors' assistance alone is far from sufficient to produce a perfect product. Despite the imperfect service, we need customers who are enthusiastic about it and give us feedback in the first place. And such customers deserve VIP treatment from the company.

When do you have the most passion on running your business? It's not long from the time when you started your business. If you don't start the sales you want to delay most at this time, the sales will get more difficult. You must become familiar with the sales process from the beginning. Don't miss the boat.

Otherwise, sales will depend on expensive ways to market later. There's another chance to focus on making perfect products. Do you want to bring the perfect product to the world? Then start selling when it isn't perfect. That is the most efficient way.

6. The power of pre-sales to strengthen the confidence of the founder.

You may be familiar with the story of Romeo and Juliet. Despite the terrible objections from both families, Romeo and Juliet loved each other and risked their lives for each other. This well-known Shakespearean tragedy was also made into lots of films and plays that are loved by the public. In fact, some psychological experiments have shown that if there are suitable opposition factors, they can deepen the love affair between lovers.

Let's think of a stream running quietly and slowly. What happens if the stream is flowing down but is suddenly blocked by a large stone? If the flow is blocked, it means that more energy and momentum are created in the reverse direction.

For about five years, I've met both with prospective entrepreneurs and current entrepreneurs every week. Combined, the people who came to large startup forums numbered well over 10,000 people. I came face to face on a one-to-one basis with more than 1,000 people. What are some of the questions I got the most from them?

Many people I met didn't know what to start with for their business and didn't know what they like. One person wanted to start a business with what they like, but they didn't know what kind of work that was. They asked many questions about how to find it.

In fact, few people who followed the Korean education system diligently are without such problems. Is there any time in the curriculum to help you discover who you are, what you like, and what you don't like? It's natural to think that only tracking grades are the most important thing unless you happen to meet the teachers who care about your inner self, not the scores or grades.

Then, how do you know what you love and what you like to do in your life? You already know the answer. You can try anything and see whether you like it or not.

But why not try it? They are afraid that once they try it or if they don't like it, they won't know the next step. That's because they're concerned they might not get acknowledgment from the people around them or from the public. Then they think they'll have wasted their time and opportunity and become more like a person who has failed. People who have taken a safe path think this way, are cautious about experiencing it in person and are sensitive about wasting precious time.

The sad thing is that we're wasting a great deal of time taking such worries and stresses with us all our lives. Such worries come only from the imagination when we think about failure. Even if you don't feel like it, or even if you're afraid of something, once you try it, you start to see things that are very different from the beginning.

In the past, I mostly concentrated on avoiding things I didn't feel like doing. On the other hand, now is different from the past. I have a welcoming approach to find what I like. And it's being passed on to the people who start their business based on this mindset. I've seen a lot of people overcome the fear and start their own business and grow it explosively.

I find it interesting that founders who didn't receive enthusiastic support from their neighbors often grew up faster than those who got support. Business items that are considered to be a natural success take the edge off the entrepreneur. Self-confidence is high and they're easily caught off guard. Suddenly, when someone hears something unexpected or goes through negative feedback, he or she is psychologically depressed. There are so many entrepreneurs who were good at first but collapsed at a small, unexpected punch.

Butterfly Investment guides prospective entrepreneurs and supports them as they start their own business even if they want to sell an unwelcome item. Through this challenge, the founders make an essential, solid preparation. As the item is ready for negative feedback, and it's not a popular item to be supported in the first place, the founder has low expectations for customer response and can endure initial difficulties while concentrating on the item's growth and improvement.

Sales should be carried out without specifying business items, and maximum response to negative feedback should be received at that time. As they develop business items in this way, and as they persuade those who respond negatively to business items, they also develop a love for and assimilation of business items.

Despite the fact that it isn't the kind of field they want to be in, many people get attached to it through this process and form a decent brand. And then they get to the point where they discover the connection between the business item and the work they want to do.

A case in point is Harulab. "Write a book in one day" is the main service of Harulab. But the CEO of Harulab also said, "At the beginning of the project, writing a book is the most difficult thing for me." However, financial issues arose, and the CEO could no longer delay business to cover expenses. She has come to think that if she succeeds in doing what is the least favorite thing for her, she'll be able to do better.

As she has been growing her business for three years, she feels that she has many ways to link her favorite fields through this project, and she has developed her business as one of the leading companies to help and guide people to write a book.

I was also unsure about a project that involved sending business ideas via email weekly for $1,100. I was afraid too, and everyone around me also said, "It doesn't make sense." They thought that I would give up soon. Nevertheless, when I heard those comments from people, I thought that it would be impossible for anyone to do it if I didn't do it. And I wanted to make it successful at all costs.

Since then, whenever Choi and I discussed making business-idea documents, I created documents just like artists create their masterpiece and tried to sell it. No matter how difficult it may be, I made a promise to myself that I would do it for at least one year. Even if I quit in the end, I was going to compliment myself by just maintaining this ridiculous business for a whole year. After a year of such concerns and opposition from friends and family, I sustained the business and even expanded it. Then, the affection for the business changed. More than anyone else, I was a man who loved my business the most, and I had more confidence in my business.

Of course, as such positive energy continued to affect the people around me, more and more people have recognized the business of Butterfly Investment. It was my daily routine to try to sell and get rejected and to organize how to answer customer questions. When I couldn't give fine answers to customers, I came home and struck the desk with regret. Then, I consulted with Choi again, read the biography of those who established the unique business, and watched the video and reorganized and refined my work.

Pre-sales aren't just about making sales first. Entrepreneurs add their affection for their business items through the pre-sales. It's to acknowledge one's skillfulness and amateurishness through pre-sales. It's a basic step to show attachment to the project and to build trust through the pre-sales. That's how you become a real businessperson and professional entrepreneur. You can become a real expert by selling in the field by yourself.

People are thrilled by the hidden endings of movies or surprises. Imagine a businessperson who doesn't seem attached to their business and product and doesn't seem professional and passionate, and is only rejected by customers. Then, suddenly one day, they talk about their business items with sparkling eyes and passion. It would be like a movie if an entrepreneur who couldn't answer customer questions that touched a sensitive spot became confident and start selling and answering questions in sophisticated language.

These are the things that the founder has to show their clients and what the founder has to gain through the pre-sales. Butterfly Investment asks, "Where in the world is the rule that only a fully equipped person can start a business and succeed?" Moreover, founders aren't asked to start selling with complete products and services.

Reid Hoffman, the co-founder of LinkedIn, said, "If you're not ashamed of your first product, you launched it too late."

I will say, "If you didn't start sales of the product before it was complete, it was too late to sell.

7. Don't try to find something that looks good. Make what you do now successful.

"Mr. Shin, I'm also preparing to start a business these days."

Many people say that, while they're working at a job, when they read my book and prepare for a new business.

"Oh, good for you. Then when do you quit your job?"

And they say, "I'm looking at one thing or another, so once I find a nice item or idea, I'm going to leave my job."

I've seen many people preparing to start their own business. However, few of them actually find great items, become successful, and leave their current job. Many people who are preparing to start a business while they're still employed take the following approach.

"I have to find something that works well while I'm working, and then quit my job."

Of course, there's no safer and tempting option than this. Nevertheless, there's something that a person who makes a safe choice needs to succeed. It's good luck. If someone makes a safe choice and becomes successful, they may be very, very lucky person. Otherwise, they became lucky because they built up the luck beforehand. To succeed, you need to put your best foot forward to build up the luck.

It's unreasonable to hope things will work out well while you just dabble in this and that while working all day at work.

"I'm working days, but it's worth trying because I get off work early, and I have time to spare on weekends." However, simply having a lot of time left doesn't mean you can spend that time entirely on preparing to start a business.

If you think that while you have a job you can prepare your own business on the side, you're under a great illusion. This is because you consume a substantial amount of energy at work. That way, even if you have free time later, it's not easy to focus on other things after work.

You might want to watch TV shows and take a rest while drinking some beer on your couch after work. You might think you'll have plenty of time the next day, so you can start preparing properly then. The same goes for weekends. You spend the weekend relaxing because you think the weekend will come again next week. Therefore, if you're working at a company and preparing for your own business at the same time, it's hard to make progress that way. More specifically, the reasons are as follows.

First, you're under the illusion that you're trying to start a business.

When you prepare to start a business this way, you continue to think that you have to do this and that while you're resting on your couch. Instead of thinking over the specific actions you need to take to start a business, you unconsciously repeat thoughts that only put pressure on yourself.

This pattern won't help you relax, but what's more regrettable is that it makes you think you're thinking enough about starting a business. That's why someone spends a year like this and then says, "I've considered it for a year." But they realize no concrete results at all, and nothing has changed.

You must dispel your illusions that you're currently working for your business. It's shameful that no action has been taken, but you have to admit it. If you're under such a delusion, you'll never dream of quitting your job when you're preparing for a new business.

Second, you might not be supported by family members and friends.

Families know when people are working hard at work. Even though they're having a hard time at work, their families are strong in supporting them. It's not easy to break that support. After some consideration, you might tell your family that you'll quit your job and start a business. Although families understand such a decision, they're worried that stable income will go away. What's reassuring for them is that you will keep your job and prepare the business at the same time. Then later, once your business is launched successfully, you'll quit your job. Up to this point, mutual trust between you and your family will not be broken.

However, you keep procrastinating about starting your own business. You don't go to the startup forum because you're tired from work. When you get home, you say that you have to rest by watching dramas because you had a hard time at work. In addition, there's no action during the weekend. Then, there will be a conflict between you and your family.

Your family will lower their hopes that you'll start a business. After all this time, if you say, "I can't stand my job any longer, so I want to start a business now," the family cannot help but have more concerns and scold you, and you can't expect support from your family any longer.

This is why people who are preparing to start a business with the spirit of "I'll leave my job if I try something else," can't help but quit their jobs, or can't make results even after starting a business.

We must change the mindset by which we approach our own business, and make the things that we do right now successful. So what should we do? What makes it happen? The answer to the first question is "do anything." The answer to the second question is "make it the end."

If you have to do anything, I recommend you sell first. Find what you want to sell, or if you want to sell something, sell it to the neighborhood first. Then, what happens? Of course, you'll be rejected. This will be embarrassing. Then you have to think about what to do to avoid embarrassment. Do you need to write more blog articles to remind yourself of the value of your product?

Should you post a review on YouTube comparing the products you want to sell with other products?'

Furthermore, as you do sales, you may find that you have no attachment to the service or product you originally wanted to sell. Then, you'll find the answers to the following questions: "What do I really like?" "What else do I hate?" "What should I do to know this?" Butterfly Investment says you should start a morning journal. Is there any other way?

You need to do something like this and have some small feedback so you can ask questions to take the next step. Do some research, find books, and listen to a lecture to help you answer those questions. You need to take those actions to move from the stage of doing anything to the stage of making it successful.

One week of acting like this will make you grow even more than just one year of thinking about it. To make one thing happen, you should repeat everything you do and record everything from the start. Such records become a great story and content, and will definitely help to attract potential customers.

It's possible to keep increasing the number of fans who say, "One day when you start a business, I'll be your first customer." It also allows you to keep your blog neighbors open to people who are interested in your business. It also makes it possible to grow Naver Cafe (a content hub, the

Korean version of Google) and other communities where people are interested in your business, without stopping halfway. You can also create a Facebook page and a Facebook group to keep posting content. Those things are the actions that make what you do now successful.

Of course, to do this, you must constantly create content and try to sell your product. Even if not a single sales event occurs, showing this step helps your family to not stop you from starting a business. Making what you do successful should be done through this process. And in order to make something successful, you should also care about energy management at your daily job.

Previously, only working at your job was what you were actually "doing." That's why you used all your energy there, but once you try to sell anything, you'll be looking for a way to save some energy. Until now, your energy wouldn't have been distributed evenly. That's because you weren't following a substantial process in preparation for starting a business as you were only looking for something that works.

Since I started my own business, I have built new content through a WordPress website, Naver Cafe, podcasts, and YouTube. I wasn't very good at ad-libbing and wasn't used to editing videos either. So what I challenged you to consider above can't be described as "If it works several times, I'll do it." When I encountered any difficulties, my choice was always "Keep doing what

I'm doing right now until its successful." In fact, I haven't stopped for years. I keep making content and upload video clips and podcast episodes, so now I have many fans and followers who continue with me today.

Mr. Cho, Jung-il, CEO of Brick Factory, who is doing business with LEGO art, said he really liked the project after receiving business-idea documents from Butterfly Investment. He wanted to earn money from artwork and quit college because he wanted to live freely. But people around him said, "This business is difficult. It doesn't pay you much. Who buys such things?"

Therefore, he was inclined to do a part-time job and develop his business if it worked well. Of course, the company didn't make progress, and Butterfly Investment stressed that he needed to be more aggressive in business to become a CEO. Since then, he has quit his part-time job and made videos about the process of making LEGO art and uploaded them online. He declared himself to be in business and immersed himself in the work to make it happen.

There wasn't much response in the beginning, but he didn't give up and continued to produce fantastic works with LEGO and continuously uploaded videos about his LEGO artwork. Based on this portfolio, he continued to promote his work and tried to sell his artwork. Increasingly, friends bought the artwork; and he received orders from new clients, signed an interior contract with a cafe, was asked to appear on a TV show, and received a collaboration proposal from a large company.

Most of the people who grow up to be entrepreneurs of zero-base startups choose to make their own ideas work. Dabbling in this or that only adds to the fact that you never get the concrete results you want. Let's stop searching for what would work. Make what you're doing successful.

8. Four typical types of customers the entrepreneur will encounter.

Knowing the four types of customers you'll meet in the field makes the sales approach easier. However, before I start talking about four types of customers, I have something to say first. It's something I have been seeing for the five years since I started, and have been experiencing almost every week with countless potential customers, in the sales field and in training sessions with startup CEOs.

You'll meet customers who have a personality similar with the founder's. If there are 100 customers, 80 of them have ideas and feelings similar to the CEO's. This is not just what I felt, but also what all of the founders I trained proved to be true. If the founder tends to be aggressive and is good at lying, such people become the customers, and the founder has a hard time with those customers.

Recognizing that the situation is attributable to the founder himself or herself will help you overcome the situation. If not, you'll get tired of arguing with customers.

I had always believed before I started my business that this is how the world works. It was an idea that I naturally acquired from the *Book of Changes* and from listening to lectures about quantum mechanics. Since then, I've tried to live a really nice and sophisticated life when I started my own business. I've tried to use positive words, as well as good manners, to put the whole situation in my favor and to make the difficult situations a factor in my growth. This has had a good effect on my life itself, but it was because I wanted to meet people who I would like and who would have similar attitudes toward people and life as well. If I maintain a positive attitude, similar people will come as my customers.

As I said earlier, I have the type of customers I want to meet. It's becoming more and more this way as time passes. It's surprising to me that even the entrepreneurs from zero-base startups who have been starting their business for two to three years are experiencing the same thing—encountering the customers who have similar characteristics to the founders'.

I wanted to tell this story first to those who are preparing to start a business and those who have started it. You need to reflect on your life as if you're living like a customer you want to meet. From now on, I will talk about the types of customers you'll meet and also discuss the attitude of entrepreneurs.

First, there's the price-obsessed customer.

This customer doesn't even go through the service you provide in detail. They simply match your services with one of the services they knew earlier. This customer focuses only on comparing the price of the similar service with the price of the service you provide. So when you try to explain the service and the product in detail, they simply tell you that they know everything, without listening to your explanation, and want you to tell them only the price.

There are entrepreneurs who think that if some customers ask only for a price, they will buy the product right away. That's a big mistake. When the appeal for the value of the product is not effective, customers simply think that any price is expensive. It's common to hear a grousing customer say a product is too expensive here when there's not much else to consider. Of course, this won't be good to hear for the founder.

Think back to what kind of customer you were. Were you bent on just hearing the price without asking any other information? If you keep starting your own business without changing your attitude, you'll meet clients similar to yourself and find this to be true.

Second, there's the negative customer.

The second type of customers doesn't have a happy face at first. This customer looks as if they'll explode if you touch their nerve a little. And they keep showing that they're the worst person in the world.

"I got annoyed because there was so much traffic on the way."

" Of course, on a day like today, my car broke down, and I have no luck at all."

"I don't want to get an education, but the company wants me to listen."

"How do I believe everything you say is true?"

Of course, you can also sell to these customers. But even if you sell to these customers, you can get into a lot of trouble afterwards. This is the case where even if the product is damaged due to customer error—the company can be held liable for the entire product—or even if they just simply change their mind after the purchase. To prevent this from happening, you can make contracts, but the contracts are likely to be useless when you meet this type of customer.

In the early stage of business, there was plenty of energy and time to actively sell to all customers, and a founder could approach even the negative customers. However, things can change. These days, many people are still asking, but I'm not actively selling to these negative customers. Even if they want to pay for it, ask them to find out more information about the services and buy later. I've discovered that those negative customers can hurt the image of countless existing customers and companies.

Let's look back on what kind of client you were. Are you being negative about everything, blaming others, and insisting on your own interests regardless of the contract? If you want to start up, even if you were negative in the past, or if you are now, you'll have to change. Otherwise, you'll mainly deal with customers like yourself.

The third type of customer is someone who's a meticulous and detail-oriented person. When they have to buy something, they gather and keep as much information as possible from the market. Before I started my own business, I used to be a customer of this type. If I found a service or product to purchase, I would watch all the reviews—all videos, and articles. In fact, it was almost as if I would make a purchase soon enough. It just took some time. Therefore, this is different from customers who take information negatively. This is a customer who actively accepts information. They open their wallet without hesitation when they have the information they want.

I'm releasing a lot of information online for free regarding zero-base startups and Butterfly Investment. In addition, I answer all of the questions asked by people who come to my session every week. There are many customers who take note of every bit of information. A meticulous customer collects all the information regardless of price, either cheap or expensive. As a founder, you want to avoid the first and second types of customers, and you want to meet the third type. They take a little time to finally purchase your goods, but this is a customer who can recognize your products on their own and make payments. They have a high satisfaction level after purchase and use the service well.

Are you a thorough customer? If so, this is not the type of customer you want to avoid. You may keep this type. Yet I have changed from this type of customer to the fourth type. And I'm seeing many customers of that type. Let me introduce the next type.

The fourth type is the price-insensitive customer.

When it comes to price-insensitive customers, only rich customers can be imagined. However, this isn't necessarily the case. This type of customer includes those who don't spare money if they truly value something. These customers have spent a lot of money on the products and services they buy. They're willing to pay if they're satisfied with a certain part of the process, even if they're not satisfied with everything.

I spent most of my money in the past on high-cost education programs. As I used them frequently, I got an eye for choosing a good program, and I realized that it was worth more than the tuition even if I took an expensive program and mastered it on my own. I still enroll in expensive programs or consulting. I spend much more than I spent in the past. Even if the education is not satisfactory overall, I can find something satisfactory there and apply it to my business right away and create more value. I've become price-insensitive because I earn more money than I did in the past, but I'm living like that because I'm the type of customer I want to meet in business.

"I just want to meet a customer like me."

This customer can speak with such dignity. They only have what they value. They're willing to pay a high price for something that is really good for them even if there are a few shortcomings. This is a real customer whom I want to meet. And I'm seeing a lot of clients like this.

What kind of customer would you like to meet? What type of customer do you live by now? You might want to avoid customer types one and two and want to meet customer types three and four, but not at the beginning of the business, during which you might need to sell to types one and two. Now, however, I want to avoid selling to types one and two. At the beginning of the business, I think it's better to approach and respond to various types of customers. Then, you can become desperate to meet customers of types three and four and change.

Of course, customer types one and two will take time, but they can change to types three and four through education or conversation. At the beginning of the business, I also took a lot of time to support clients who were types one and two. And it made me desperately need types three and four.

As I've said over and over again, nothing is more certain than the type of customer you want to meet, as you act first. I know this might sound like a superstition, and it might sound like words from a book on spirituality. This phenomenon might not be fully understood at first, but once believed, it can be real. I'm experiencing it myself and with my co-entrepreneurs. So I believe this because I've confirmed it in my reality.

9. There is no meaningless work done in vain.

I spent more than two years preparing for the exam to become a government officer in Korea. My mid-twenties were like a golden time for me, and it was the most energetic time. After failing the exam, it seemed like a completely meaningless time and a total failure. Nevertheless, I changed my mind, and then it became a big opportunity to plan the decades ahead of me. If I had passed and lived a stable life, I never would have experienced the fantastic moments of freedom and love that I'm experiencing right now.

And if I hadn't tried for the exam, my parents would have consistently pushed me to take it, and whatever I did besides the exam, I would have had a burden on my mind. I think I was able to meet a bold challenge because I was able to put the burden down completely because I failed the exam.

I became a sales representative because I wanted to start a totally new thing after the exam, and made efforts to get away from that, spending time and money to learn sales. At first, I felt like a failure. What I thought was right was later discovered to be wrong. I felt like I was only stepping on mines in a minefield.

But if I hadn't experienced this period in my life, what I am now wouldn't exist. To motivate myself, I read books and listened to lectures by the authors. While meeting with those who had founded their businesses and worked themselves into the ground, I learned ways to overcome extreme situations. I trained daily to give meaning to each moment and recognize that there are always elements to be thankful for, even if they appear to be unfortunate. As a result, my previous acts that were considered as meaningless in the past changed and appeared in a new light.

I was once into spam marketing. Since 2010, I had been chasing various ways to earn money. Then, I entered the marketing world, and I had to go all the way to the end so I could meet the relevant leaders and experts of the field. Back then, spam marketing was the most exciting for me. There were a lot of ways to apply it. When a new program came out, I bought it and tried it right away. I had strategically posted articles and applied SEO so they would get top exposure. Several blogs were discarded after I tried new things. But as time went by, I felt that I was involved in the repetition of meaningless things. Although there are some people around who have made a name in the field, they're also busy competing with each other and cutting one another down. The competition over who is better at spam marketing was not a good thing either. I thought that spam marketing would make a lot of money for me, so I spent a lot of time making the content. In the end, however, I decided to leave that field.

When I was into spam marketing, I practiced writing like crazy. I lived with the engine running in my head, trying to figure out what words people respond to and what cognitive steps they make to purchase. After losing interest in spam marketing, I found the importance of authentic content and good luck. Thus, I was able to combine the knowledge of spam marketing with the steady action of building luck. Then, I had a chance to be recognized by solving the problems of people who have branding but can't make money yet.

Events and programs were disappearing because they didn't promote effectively. Only a few people were involved, and they began to breathe and revive with channels that I run. I also have a history of selling dozens of travel package services worth 1 million won (approximately $1,000) only one week before the travel departure date, solely with one blog article.

I didn't blame the meaningless attempts of the past and started to believe that those attempts were stepping-stones for my personal growth. I suffered psychological setbacks due to failing the government exam, and the mental and counseling experiences I went through to overcome them had begun to serve as a career that could encourage those who are struggling to start a business. There are people who don't ignore the previous attempts and shortcomings and start to embrace and appreciate them. In my life, there are people who pay for my time to listen to that story.

People who are preparing to start their own business are encouraged to start selling right away while producing content related to their favorite items. In this process, the founders will go through massive attempts and trial and error. Their product doesn't sell right away. It's also common for many months to pass by. However, people who keep trying at this stage will have value per hour. The know-how and content accumulated during the process will be returned to their own branding. On top of that, I'm helping them to grow the scale of sales little by little by working together to generate meaningful traffic to their content.

First of all, a new entrepreneur should know how to make money out of their accumulated know-how, examples, and coaching skills. They should experience a lot of setbacks while meeting with many people of all different types of personalities, and grow their own capacity. Without that process, if they start a team right away because they're good at ideas, get an investment, and then start marketing, they may earn money in the beginning, but there might be a moment when not only individuals but also the entire company is in crisis because of incidents that stress the cracks of personal growth that they have ignored.

However, attempts to satisfy the opinions of others have limitations in bringing about personal growth and business. If you try something to raise your own voice that looks meaningless at first, you don't have to regret it. You can find meaning, of course. More tries, calling you crazy by people around you, and ignorance will teach you. In the process, you can gradually gain the ability to dig yourself out and find enjoyment in your life. Those who are seeking to start a zero-base startup keep trying many things. Start selling before the item becomes specific. It's a great attempt that creates wealth from nothing.

There are people who have created something completely out of nothing and these people have their own view of the world. They believe that they can make money if they have marketing know-how without having any other experience. I keep warning them. Of course, only one out of 10 people listens. They don't want trial and error. The trials, when they were pushed around in the past, are mistaken for a meaningful experience. If it is because of a trial someone self-defines as a victim, they still haven't been able to dig properly or find meaning.

Maybe some people are too tired to speak out their own voice. There will be a lot of people around you who will ask you to stop trying meaningless things. There might even be someone beside you who tells you to wake up and live like everyone else. Such an environment has actually existed around you all your life which can be controlled so just be whatever you want.

Nevertheless, you can always change the meaning of what you do as good and bad. How can you think of living in a different environment when the people around you just set everything for you in your life? How can you dream new dreams and develop a new life?

Destroy the shovel that the world has forced into your hands and take out your own shovel now. Start using your own shovel. Keep providing solid and positive meaning for what you do now. Your time will be worth it, and others will be willing to start buying your time at high prices.

When you make yourself valuable and realize the value of your own time by trying different things, you expand your business or build a team. Spread the spirit of your new shovel to the people around you. What you build won't fall apart from most attacks. I support all of your trials. Be sure to remember: There is no such thing as a meaningless attempt.

10. The limits of writing 100 times and how to overcome them.

In Chinese characters, the word "faith" literally means "believe in an idea or thought." To think is one thing, and to believe in thought is another. What should we do to believe in our thoughts? You can find hints in everyday life. We believe that people who see each other often, people who interact over time, and people who go through all kinds of ups and downs will continue to see each other. Then, the way to believe thoughts is naturally inferred.

If several times you think that you want to believe in something, you will actually believe it. And you can call it faith. To think of your future wannabe self frequently has become a favorite part of self-development and motivation courses. It's often talked about that you can achieve what you want if you think of it often, but there aren't many details about how to think. It's hard to think of what you want. Things continue to come up in our daily lives, causing distracting thoughts to arise. Problems to be solved in your daily life take priority in your thoughts. Therefore, it's become popular to write the image of what you want 100 times.

I also remember a long time ago, when I was a salesman, I felt heartened every day through this time of 100 writings. I still see a lot of people who say they've achieved the goals they want through writing 100 times. Some people keep picturing ideas over and over again through this process; however, only doubt grows, not faith. Then there are some side effects: They blame themselves for their lack of effort or feel disappointed believing they're not worthy of success. Why does this happen, and how can we overcome it?

Contrary to what you might think, the act of creating faith through a picture of the future breaks your faith. Some feel their future well and others do not.

It depends on the environment, education, and culture an individual has experienced. What are the characteristics of people who say that they achieved their goals through writing 100 times? They can draw an action plan to achieve that goal automatically and naturally through 100 writings. Who is the person whose action plans are drawn automatically? They have tried many things many times before and have experienced small failures and successes repeatedly in their life. Because they naturally learned how things work and how people do independent things, action plans are drawn automatically.

Who would be more likely to think of the detailed action plan—someone sitting at the desk or someone experiencing real problems in the field? Wouldn't those who travel to strange places and face unexpected situations, who have had the chance to interact with strangers and meet all kinds of different people with various emotions, and who have met various teachers and faced impossible missions on the ground have more specific action plans to encounter certain situations?

Those who say they've achieved their goal only through 100 writings are those who automatically find action plans when thinking about their future. So while writing down their goals for the future, they have no resistance or doubt at all. However, if beginners, businessmen, and college students who have never lived an action-based life in the past blindly imitate the practice of writing 100 times, they'll continue to bump into their own minds. Suspicion reiterates and claims that self-development is useless. There is something to be done before writing down the picture 100 times. Write down what you have to do first to achieve what you want to be.

If a person who's new to starting a business is dreaming about starting a business and read my previous book and the words *I Work Only Four Hours a Week and Earn 10 million Won a Week,"* and starts writing 100 times, he or she will face the limit soon. It's difficult to relate any word in this sentence to reality. My advice is to write down a course of action or detailed action plan step by step 100 times instead of writing the result that you want.

For example, one of my recommendations is "articles 100, videos 100."

The goal is to write 100 articles related to the business you're working on, create 100 videos, and accomplish the goal of "working four hours a week and earning 10 million won."

To accomplish this plan, you must constantly read books, go to relevant lectures and seminars, and meet potential customers. And you should continue to create your own content. You can continue to check your action progress by writing 100 times, and link it with everyday life. Once you achieve this action plan, a different future will come along naturally. You'll meet your fans and prospective customers. There will be publishing offers from publishing companies, and you'll receive requests for seminars and conferences like TEDx Talks. Of course, your competence and capacity will be improved, and you'll think better of the future through your experience.

After this phase, write down the goal of "working four hours a week and finally making 10 million won." However, if you still have some doubts, you can train while writing down another action plan. Simply repeating the abstract idea of what you want to be in the future will only make you worry about how the process should be achieved and will lead to confusion. This is a common situation if there's no detailed plan. Under these circumstances, there's no need to blame others for your own lack of will or to envy those who are doing well.

Picturing your dream requires training. There's no need to blame beginners for not finishing the 42.195-kilometer marathon. Isn't it natural to try running one kilometer first? Walking and running are all too simple and familiar, but people take it for granted that they should take steps slowly and train first to run the marathon.

On the other hand, concepts such as imagining, believing, and achieving what you want aren't familiar, nor are they completely defined by detailed guides. There's no place to deal with the importance of training in these areas, even though training is a necessary part because it's unfamiliar. Without training, people produce vague failures and develop theories about the uselessness of self-development.

Since I also thought in the past that self-development is useless, I want to point out the importance of it. I also thought I was a loser, but I was wrong. Anyone who takes the proper steps can achieve what they want.

I'm sure there are people who thinks the same way. Many times, I was frustrated, but I finally found an easier step and took it slowly to achieve my present success. I was able to experience various things while starting my own business through pre-sales. And as I was teaching this way of starting a business, I could see more people having the same experience as me and achieving their beliefs.

Picturing your dream with a strong belief is a very difficult task. Nonetheless, it's not impossible at all. In particular, the task can accelerate much faster when taking new experiences and various actions that haven't been done in the past. This is because new experiences empower the strength of imagination and thoughts.

11. The secret of imagination to dramatically increase sales capabilities.

Napoleon was born in a colony of France, but became the emperor of France, leading many wars to victory. Why did Napoleon with various adverse conditions excel at war and winning? You can find the answer in his pre-war ritual.

Napoleon was said to meditate before a war. To put it in a more understandable way, one can say that he envisioned an imaginary time. So what did he imagine? Did he imagine losing the war? I guess not. He repeatedly imagined winning the war. He led the victory in real life, as he had imagined. In this regard, Napoleon even demonstrated that imagination dominates the world.

You may have heard a lot about the fact that the human brain can't distinguish between imagination and reality. I'm also building a process through the power of imagination that others said was impossible. Despite my introverted personality traits, I used imaginary training to maximize my sales capabilities. It was also possible to sell incomplete products and not be swayed by repeated rejections, but rather to maximize my individual growth.

Anyone who's interested in self-improvement might have heard about the power of imagination as described in the extremely popular book *The Secret* by Rhonda Byrne. However, this simple message is not enough: "Imagine what you want vividly." Although I tried hard to imagine what I wanted, I could hardly see what was happening in real life and only experienced more disappointment.

Therefore, you should not just imagine without proper guidance. Imagination needs practice. It's not easy for modern people to practice a happy imagination as they unconsciously respond negatively to countless external stimuli every day. Imagination is also associated with questioning power. Asking questions is like practicing a new imagination beyond the existing limits. Someone who's good at asking questions has a good imagination. It's a very natural process.

However, how long have we had to ask questions through the education system in Korea? Would it be difficult and confusing to tell someone young with no real experience let their imagination be free and imagine their success? If they were stressed and extremely nervous, asking them to imagine the successful future would be bound to have negative side effects as they'd unconsciously think only of negative images in their daily life. Some people say they've succeeded in just this way, but they're mostly pure people, frequent practitioners of meditation, artists, people who usually do a lot of daydreaming, or people who ask questions.

We must be prepared to accept the imagination first. You should start by observing naturally emerging thoughts, not by forcing your imagination. There are so many thoughts that pass by without reflecting on them. You must have time to acknowledge them.

When we unconsciously empathize with every image we think of, we consume a lot of energy. In order to generate positive thoughts and get the right feeling at the moment, one must first be able to select the thoughts that come to mind.

We know that we can get to our destination quickly by riding in a car, but it's dangerous to give a driver a car key when he or she doesn't have a license. Imagination is like a car that gets to its destination quickly. However, it's difficult to imagine positively and to feel the entire emotion through such an imagination. No one has a license to drive their imagination. Instead of getting a license, you should first make friends with the imagination.

The training to observe the aforementioned ideas is also called Vipassana meditation. I always try to stay awake. Therefore, I'm diligent in practicing meditation in daily life and sincerely recommend meditation to those who want to start a business. I believe meditation gives you a better chance to imagine positively and allows you to find the opportunity to train your mind every day through your new business. (Other parts of this book deal in more detail with the idea of starting a business connecting to mental training.)

Through Vipassana meditation, you can go through a phase of getting to know your thoughts and ask questions to get to know them. When you get close to your thoughts, you're ready to become close to your imagination.

When I give a lecture, I deliberately lead people to ask questions. This process helps them get used to imagining things at ease. It's hard at first, but it gets easier. However, it's not necessary to ask questions only in lectures.

You can ask many questions while reading. Reading a book can be like talking to a writer. Reading naturally raises questions and makes it easier to imagine things related to the book subject. You may wonder if you have to pay attention to these things when you want to sell well. If you know a subject only vaguely, you have more to worry about. I really want to let more people know how to harness the power of imagination.

I've met a lot of people who wanted to use their imagination to improve sales skills, but they couldn't learn how to imagine them properly, so they had a lot of unnecessary worries. Your ability to imagine is improved by daily life and getting used to observing thoughts and questions in books you read and lectures you attend. Without these processes, it's difficult to direct your imagination positively.

The practice of meditation in daily life allows you to selectively accept feelings. Training to ask questions through books allows you to acquire a lot of imaginary material. When these things penetrate into everyday life, you aren't forced to imagine, but naturally imagine what you want.

It's easier to imagine in a comfortable situation, instead of forcing your body under strain and stress. As soon as someone wakes up in the morning, he or she can imagine what he or she wants to look like in a state closer to the unconscious just like before going to bed at night. This is because you include your imagination in your daily routine, and while you sleep, you enter your unconscious mind.

Examples of explosive sales growth and a surge in sales through imagination training are mentioned in various books. I'm such a case, and I'm seeing such growth through the founders whom I'm guiding in starting their own businesses. There's an imaginary training step to further improve sales performance. And if they aren't fully aware of it properly, it can reduce sales performance.

The process of pre-sales isn't an easy one; it's a series of hardships. If you follow this process through your imagination, what happens in your head? Yes, it's easy to think of images that hurt and are constantly rejected. But having negative imagination and trying to respond positively and give feedback can be effective.

However, if you continue this method from the beginning, you'll bring to mind only elements that you can't carry out, and you'll experience side effects that will prevent you from taking action. So what should you do? You must also try to imagine in reverse order. In other words, you have to think about the success of sales first. You should first imagine choosing success and feeling your happy feelings from achieving success. If you imagine success first, and then go back to problems that are blocked, you can simulate the problems with positive emotions.

Obviously, sales capabilities can be improved through imagination. It changes the image within the unconscious, and it affects your reality. However, if you aren't familiar with the guidance mentioned here and focuses only on positive imagination, you'll reject it at the conscious stage. If you collide with the unconscious, your body will become heavier, your feelings will be negative, and you'll be in a vicious cycle.

I'm a person who has suffered from being in this situation for a long time. Thus, to go to the next level, I spent much time and money on expensive lectures, foreign books, and video courses related to this. I was tested first and verified with actual changes in my current outlook and sales growth. And I went offline to give guidance in some of these areas and witnessed people's sales growth explode.

Read this part calmly again. It's obvious that this story will lead to sales growth. It's sad that nobody can tell the secret of imagination properly. If one knows something vaguely, it will only interfere with performance. At the end of this chapter, I would like to say something related to Napoleon, just as he left a word of praise for his imagination.

Through imagination, anyone can improve sales skills. Imagination can rule the world.

12. Peace of mind vs. sales growth, a delicate correlation.

I use Google Analytics and analyze users' activity patterns on the webpage. Facebook ads can be set as targets and provide information about which content is better, which content goes viral better, and which conversion rates are better.

You can send an email to customers and do an A/B test—which compares two versions of a webpage, email, or app to check which works better—to determine which email is effective in converting to sales, and which email the customer responds to better. It's also possible to analyze which titles of e-mails are more effective and more frequently opened by customers. We're living in a world where we can analyze all of our results with data, and if we choose better options when responding, our sales will be increased.

But the part I want to talk about in this chapter is far from data. Rather, it's a story of extremes. I want to say that peace of mind greatly affects sales revenue. While it's possible to get numbers to quantify data, there's no number we can apply to peace of mind. There's no way to correctly determine if there's a point where the mind is directly connected to sales. It belongs to the invisible realm.

If you relate to what I've written above, then you'll understand the following: "When I feel peaceful, I have a warmer smile on my face and gain trust so I sell better." This means that I bring the result to an area that's not visible.

I've been running a business that people say isn't normal. It's to sell ideas for zero-base startup businesses and spread the spirit of starting them. No one sold business ideas online without a patent, but no one thought it would be possible.

Even I wouldn't be doing this if I hadn't had a great change in my thinking through Choi. Therefore, the history of Butterfly Investment that I've been walking on has been nothing more than digging through the forest. Along the way, half-doubtful and half-anticipatory entrepreneurs emerged, and they're also promoting their names by developing creative business ideas learned from Butterfly Investment.

Once you start a business, you're lonelier than you anticipated. This is because it's hard to find people who'll fully support you. And starting a business is hard. This is because people often get misunderstood and abused. It's a natural thing to happen when you have a business, and although you can't get rid of it, you can think of it as a fun challenge.

Certain customers complain about their attempts to be better for the overall customer. Those who accept your authority and know you best can attack you most painfully. The more emotional interactions you have with a customer, the more sadness and pain they can make you feel. The ability to be sympathetic is good for entrepreneurs, but it can also be a serious disadvantage.

When a customer who initially shares empathy stops sharing it, the salesperson feels very isolated. As the number of customers increases and business expands, it's not easy to maintain the same level of empathy with all customers. Some people come up to your face, gather all the information they need, and then turn dark the next day to complain.

One of the things I thought was good for doing business was discovering there are many different kinds of people in the world. I found out that people have a range of qualities, and are not all good or all bad. I also learned that there's nothing better than looking and nothing worse than looking.

Therefore, I'm telling people who are preparing to start a business without capital that it's better to think of it as a process of mental training. Since they can experience an active life and perform their mind training while earning money through their business, I believe there's no challenge more valuable than starting one's own business.

Interestingly, there are people who solve problems arising from management through mental training, and there are many books written by such people. For example, there's Michael Singer's book, *The Surrender Experiment: My Journey into Life's Perfection*. Rather than focus on solving the problem physically, he wrote a book that tells the story of a problem he solved by simply looking at his own heart and mind and releasing uncomfortable feelings.

I was really surprised when I read this book. His way to solve business problems is very much like my way. I was reluctant to tell people that I was doing business with this spirit, but he wrote this book proudly and showed that many people were sympathetic to it.

Likewise, in my first book, I mentioned that I'm using Ho'oponopono. It was my approach to considering that the origin of various problems before me was a lump of emotion that had not been resolved within me. So I've been doing business believing that my efforts to purify my mind will help solve the problems before me and create more sales beyond that.

As I mentioned earlier, when you do business, it doesn't just happen to be pleasant most of the time. From an objective point of view, there are many things that are unpleasant. But if you respond to them emotionally all the time, only the negative energies build up. You can easily blame others, don't think of yourself, lose open-mindedness, and miss out on creative solutions.

If you drink a lot of alcohol to release your stress, or if you become a bad mouth, or you curse, your body will be damaged, and at the same time, you'll lose your confidence. Then your mood will be ruined even more. In many cases, business owners repeat this vicious cycle. If you keep people who speak ill of you, who are mean to you, and people who have different faces inside, you'll get nervous, you won't be able to focus on your work, and you'll act in a way that does nothing to help sales.

On the contrary, if you try to bring peace to your mind, something strange happens. The person who hurt my feelings is actually the one who helps me outperform, and the one who doesn't appreciate me is the one who reminds me that I don't appreciate someone important. A dissatisfied customer is a grateful person who helps me upgrade my products to another level. At first, it can be difficult to think this way. But I've experienced this myself for years. I've meditated since 1998, and in particular, I sought more meditation to overcome the constant negative perception others had of me, as I wasn't going in a typical direction after graduation. I've had a long practice of observing and separating emotions from thoughts. After I started my own business, the need for meditation increased by 10 times, and the meditation has worked.

As such, there were many misunderstandings and challenges since the launch of Butterfly Investment. Of course, because I've incorporated them positively within me, I've become what I am now, and I'm living so well that I seem to have come here without any problems in my life. But thanks to Butterfly Investment, meditation was so much appreciated. I had some amazing experiences after I tried to purify my mind and release it of stress and emotions. Every time, I had an amazing experience while doing meditation that brought peace of mind. At first, I thought it was a coincidence. However, it wasn't a coincidence anymore but a rule, because it has repeated this pattern for five years without any deviations.

When sales aren't available due to hard feelings, we can review the marketing direction and change our opinion. But especially when I worked hard to clean up my mind, more sales were generated. When I asked for forgiveness and said the words "I love you" to someone who was hard on me, a payment message was displayed when the mobile phone alarm rang.

In some cases, I found it hard to make more sales for a long time, and I was unconsciously blaming others. Not long after finding out that it was my problem and spending time looking at negative emotions and releasing them, I experienced as positive as what had previously been felt as a negative. When I say this, I know there are many people who will find it strange. But people who have seen me up close have actually witnessed this.

Through this story, one out of ten people will try this and solve their own problem. So I am telling my story. It's up to the individual to accept this story or not. Nevertheless, I hope you enjoy the special pleasure of starting a business with peace of mind with meditation as I continue to experience it.

13. To the founders who wouldn't sell.

Incubating a salespreneur who's starting a zero-base startup is the biggest mission for Butterfly Investment. We're conducting regular education programs and operating a community to develop an ecosystem that can generate synergy among businesspeople. Some of them already have their own business and participate in the program with their own startup items. In this case, it's helpful to guide them to check whether an item has its own voice.

If someone doesn't have a business item yet, we help them draw the item from the abstract by giving guidelines that lead to a hidden desire and need of that person. This process makes it much easier to clarify their own business model because Butterfly Investment provides more than 50 specific business-model documents to them.

Butterfly Investment sends out a weekly letter of motivation that mentions entrepreneurship, salespreneurship, emotional control, and action plans. What's not in writing is made as video lectures and shared with membership customers.

While this program alone has grown into a great sales agent, often it's not. So the people who follow the mission of Butterfly Investment and make sales, conduct lectures and seminars, and write books can then use the next step to receive feedback or help with other services.

Because there's a story people can't talk about before a certain stage and only can in the next stage, Butterfly Investment induces their action to proceed with as many steps as possible.

Some members of Butterfly Investment make several attempts at an early stage but aren't doing well and feel lost. Butterfly Investment asks them to look objectively at where they are in. We let them know there are many other things they haven't tried yet, and introduce other approaches. It's a great pleasure and a great feeling for me to advise the actual clients to do better and improve. Normally, it's all pleasure, but sometimes I'm a bit embarrassed and confused when I hear the following.

"I can't sell my products."

"I tried to sell it, but people don't buy it. I can't do it anymore."

This is the case when they didn't start their business with their own need or desire, or if they aren't aware of the problem fully. Or they have yet to make enough attempts to get a response from clients.

It takes a long time for the market to recognize a new business even if an entrepreneur thinks it's a necessary service or product for the market, but when there are few places to provide it properly. The reaction of the market will come slowly at first. None of the items of the companies that were created together with Butterfly

Investment started amid cheers from the market. Nevertheless, because they offered items for the founders to solve their own problems or needs, most of the products have continued to sell for a year or two and developed the business. No matter how they're struggling at first, they don't say, "I can't sell my products." Or, "I've tried to sell it, but people don't buy it. I can't do it anymore."

What's the difference between those who don't talk about these things and those who give up easily? It's the conviction about their business item. More specifically, it's the conviction that their item is helpful and beneficial to someone in the world. Those other people are saying they can't sell anymore because they're not sure if their business item is useful to someone.

Entrepreneurs must be confident that their products will help themselves as well as their clients to solve problems in their life or fulfill their needs. Therefore, they don't give up on sales. If you think the world in which you are selling goods and the world in which you stopped selling is not going to be much different, sales can't be fun.

"I'll promote the spirit of zero-base startups and create and sell items that can be created without any capital. So let's make sure people don't start a business unless it's done in the way of zero-base startup. That way, people can recover easily even if they fail at first and go bankrupt."

This idea allowed me to continue selling the membership program of Butterfly Investment because I believed there was a huge difference between the world where I continued to sell and the world where I didn't. In the past, if someone had preached this salespreneurship, people wouldn't have gone bankrupt, and their families wouldn't have been disbanded.

Bae Ha-Yeon, CEO of the Coommlifegames, said, "After graduation and entering society, I was frustrated as I didn't get recognized properly. I was passionate and worked hard, but I didn't understand why I should be treated like this and had a hard life." People around her had high expectations, but she found that she lacked appeal to the world.

In that situation, she met me at the offline talk show in Korea, and she received a mission from me to write in her journal for 100 days. What she wrote was short, but she didn't miss one day. It helped her find confidence and had a positive impact on her world. Then she published her journals as a book. She experienced a life-changing process, so she made this process into a business and founded Coommlifegames. Had it not been commercialized, many young people would have been led away by the voice of the outside world instead of listening to their own inner voice.

Kang Tae-min, CEO of YoutheStar Entertainment, said, "My dream and career have changed through the stage I once stood in, in high school." He changed his major when he was in third grade (equivalent to high school in the US), majored in practical music, and later worked as a vocal trainer. While working as a vocal trainer, he wanted to create his own business and found his business items at Butterfly Investment. It's a business producing songs and records, making music videos, and holding concerts for ordinary people. If an individual is prepared to create a business, he or she is mistaken that it would cost at least 10 million won. YoutheStar Entertainment made it possible at a much lower cost. When people hold a concert with YoutheStar Entertainment, all of their friends and family come and watch them singing their songs and enjoy this together.

YoutheStar Entertainment provides services in packages and has a win-win situation with music-related businesses. Customers feel thrilled as they're treated like real stars by their friends and family. Sales for YoutheStar Entertainment can't be stopped. The world since the launch of YoutheStar Entertainment is different from the world before it.

If the person who's looking to start a business feels that there's no difference between the world of continuing sales and the world of not selling that product, he or she can complain: "I'm not going to be able to sell it. I've tried to sell it, but people don't buy it."

This is because they can start the process of finding the item from inside themselves. Or they can put more color into their existing items and make their own story. The entrepreneurs grumble because they don't want to persuade the customers. It's like asking a customer to convince them.

You may not be able to sell your content and business quickly because you're not stylish enough to show your authenticity to the world around you. In order to go to the next step, you need to continue to sell with effort and take action. That's because you get a hint from such a sales field that tells you the answer you want.

Although I recommend a new business item to people, they don't have to follow my way, and they can use it any way they want to or modify it to fit their style and situation. Most importantly, the certainty of the business is that the founder himself or herself must have it. They don't have to believe 100 percent. A positive answer to the question would be enough: "Is there any change in the world by continuing and stopping this business?" If you decide it has a certain meaning to change the world through the business, you can continue to be confident even if the current sales revenue is low. Butterfly investment has also been operating on its own meaning. That perspective makes it possible to keep going and pursue what you are doing right now. Through this motto, there are many successful companies: Never give up.

If you like this book, please leave your honest review on Amazon.

These reviews really help me as an author to get my book in front of more people just like you. Thank you!

Chapter 3. Salespreneurship action.

1. we are selling 500-dollar pencils.

The press often reports about a detailed analysis on the cost of a cup of coffee in the name of its true value. The cost of beans to make a cup of americano varies from brand to brand, but it's usually said to cost from 40 cents to 50 cents a cup.

In this respect, the cost of ingredients is only about 10 percent of americano. In price analysis, water isn't included in the cost calculation either. Adding up the price of a paper cup can also be said to cost less than the cost of an americano.

The news on cosmetics is also one of the cases most talked about. There are several companies that sell products at significantly higher margins for or against actual cost. But if the taste of the coffee is too bad for the price, or if the skin doesn't improve after using cosmetic products, consumers will know about it immediately and won't buy these products again.

However, misleading consumers and businesses to judge a company's products only based on the cost of all the materials could lead to further misunderstanding.

Consider the coffee mentioned above as an example. It's true that coffee beans and water are used as ingredients. But there's a natural added cost to making the product accessible to customers so they can savor and enjoy the coffee, such as delivering and roasting, and other expenses, such as employee paychecks and interior expenses.

Let's think about it further. What's required to set up the coffee shop? First, you need a machine that can make coffee. Just because you have a machine, doesn't mean you can get coffee automatically. It takes a skilled barista and other staff to serve good coffee to customers. And we also need a cozy place for our customers to savor the coffee. You should also pay for the interior to make your coffee shop nice and comfortable for enjoying coffee. Electric bills, water bills, and heating bills are also important factors to consider.

On top of that, the costs of making a cup of coffee worthwhile are actually unknown. Consequently, it's necessary to give an additional explanation to those articles that simply compare the price of coffee to the cost of the materials. Some people might start a business for fun and to serve people, but many more people do it to make a living. They start their business not as a gift donation, but as a profit-producing endeavor. It's quite natural that margins are included in the price in addition to cost.

Customers who are focused only on the cost of materials are easily confused by margins. The world is full of products you don't understand if you just compare the price with the cost of raw materials. We can look at luxury items as examples of such cases.

For instance, luxury bags are priced that's difficult to justify only considering the cost of materials. But many people buy the bags at that price without any objections.

But what would you think if you had to pay about $500 for a pencil? The cost of the pencil would be way less than a tenth of that. You would just laugh at such a pencil and the service of sharpening it if it was given at $500.

In fact, there's a book called *How to Sharpen Pencils*. It was an Amazon bestseller, and it was translated into Korean and sold well there as well.

In fact, this book gives the humorous view of how to sharpen a pencil. It's a very thin book. In three years, no one at my lecture said they would buy such a book.

David Rees, the author of this book, has a job at which he sharpens and sells pencils. More people are now looking for a pencil ever since they started this business, so the business keeps its prices high. David Rees is a man who studies while he enjoys sharpening a pencil.

And depending on the pencil user, he takes pride in his business as he sharpens his custom pencil. He also sends the powder from the cut of the pencil to the person who purchased the pencil to celebrate. Even the waste dust is used to add value to his product. Isn't it amazing?

With his unique humorous attitude, David Rees uploads videos on YouTube about how to sharpen the pencils, and viewers can see his special pencil-cutting devices and a variety of knives as well. People might point a finger at him, but he continues to create content that will keep viewers entertained. The content has grown so much that *The New York Times* interviewed David Rees, and the response was explosive.

It's a phenomenon that could never occur at a cost to market. After all, it's hard to say that the music and electronic books we listen to also include the cost of raw materials. The cost of distributing such digital goods is also near zero. Media like smartphones, tablets, and PCs that carry these costs are already everywhere.

The reason for paying for digital products is the effort of the creators at the time the products are produced. It's value for the time they invest. The cost can also include the value of the equipment they use. Consumers are paying for the creators' own voices and their typing hours. Consumers are buying products that are close to zero in terms of materials costs. People are paying 10 times, 100 times, and 1,000 times the cost.

When people see a product and are used to calculating costs, they naturally turn on the calculator inside their head and don't react sensitively when costs don't add up. Media reports that make the product focus on price-to-value have taken away the chance that consumers can see the real value.

In the world, outrageous products are being sold in a variety of ways. Some people are enthusiastic about the services that other people call fraud, and they're willing to pay high prices. To make selling easier, the founder of the business who makes the choice to easily lower the price in order to generate more sales has a mentality more like a consumer's than a manufacturer's.

These people are under the illusion that more people will feel valued if they lower their prices. Such choices aren't beneficial to the founder, or to the consumer, who considers quality important. The founder misses the opportunity to sell the valuable product at its proper price. Because they don't get paid, they lose the power and resources to make more valuable products and don't stay in business long. Consumers who value the product are in a situation where they can't buy it as the company doesn't make it any longer.

You shouldn't decide to bring down your prices only with short-term forecasts. Why are expensive products sold all over the world? The founders must be constantly aware of this. It must be recognized that lowering the price isn't the only way to survive the competition, but rather it brings more competition.

In other words, they will continue to make such products and go on the worst path to compete in price competitions. The goal of startups should be to create a product whose customers see it as high value and to offer it a price that will enable it to continue to be produced. And if the price is high, then the right approach is to add value to the product, but not to be hasty in choosing to lower the price.

Since this book deals with how to increase your value, let's make it easy to move on to the next page.

2. Sell proudly; create real value.

If you take other people's sales processes for granted, and you're used to taking money out of your wallet, getting money from your clients can be awkward and inconvenient.

We call this process "a sale." It makes me feel uncomfortable to imagine taking money out of someone else's wallet. It's uncomfortable to feel like you're pushing to someone a product you don't think is necessary. Making a profit from a margin feels like cheating and committing a crime.

It's a rewarding feeling that entrepreneurs might experience in the initial stage of the business when they're unaccustomed to selling the products. It may be hard to start a business and make money if you're not aware of these inconveniences and try to ignore the feeling because you'll always feel uneasy even if you earn money. There are so many people who do business while dodging the hassle of getting paid. They'd like to ask clients to pay for it, but at the moment the salesperson talks about it, they continue to delay asking for money because they don't want to look like a mercenary.

If you open a chicken restaurant and your friends come and eat there, you can't easily tell your friends to pay for their meal. Even if someone asks, "Is the boss paying for the food today?" it's hard to say no as a restaurant owner to your friends. However, it's also awkward to receive money from other acquaintances. I understand this feeling better than anyone else, and I'm the one who changed myself after I started my own business. So I never eat for free when an acquaintance opens up a new restaurant. I say I'll never visit his restaurant if they give a meal for free. And then I'll tell them to receive the payment proudly from families and friends because they received it from me.

Somebody needs to break the vicious cycle. There are more examples of people who can't proudly ask for money while providing services and products. (This might be because of certain cultural values.) Another example is the continuing practice of free seminars when they shouldn't be free. (Not all free lectures or seminars are like that. I also give free lectures sometimes.)

People who give many paid lectures sometimes give free lectures to the public, but this isn't always the case. They enjoy offering free lectures because they want to share the story with more people. But there's a problem if you give only free lectures because you can't ask for money.

I think it's beautiful to give away for free the valuable information you have learned. But people who have given free lectures know that almost half of the people who have signed up for free classes are eventually going to be no-shows.

Why is that? Since it's free anyway, people don't feel as if they could lose money even if they don't go. They don't have any obligation to show up. As a result, free lectures are expected to gain only half-participation no matter how many attendees are present. If the price of the venue is high, the lecturers continue to suffer deficits while giving free lectures. Some places lend free lecture rooms for startups, but many times, the lecturers can't afford to rent them at their preferred time.

The problem is that the attendance rate is falling because the lecture is free, but it's also very likely that the participants have a different mindset when they attend free seminars. They expect only so much from a free lecture. Even if there are good things they can't otherwise easily hear, participants sometimes aren't likely to feel the value of the lecture because it's free. But those who are appreciative of having taken a good class for free are those who will listen to and absorb any lecture.

If you don't pay for it, there's a limit to the value of the lecture. Even if you tell the same story in the lecture, the person who paid for it will ask more questions in the class, organizing the lecture when they go home, and review it to better understand it. Once again, if they pay for the seminar, they try to see the true value of what they paid for.

I don't even borrow books. I buy them and read them. If somebody I know publishes a book, and they offer me a free copy as a friend, I still pay for the book. I often buy 10 books at once. Even if they give free copies, I pay, no matter what. It's for the author's sake, but it's the only way I can read the books greedily as well as feel the books are precious and not treat them carelessly. Strangely enough, free books are easily laid aside. Why is that? Because I didn't pay for them, so I don't feel the real value properly, and they're easy to forget.

Students who work part-time while attending college to pay their tuition usually don't skip their classes. They love their classes because they paid for them with their hard-earned money. Therefore, this could lead to a virtuous cycle during which they learn more and more as they truly understand the value of the classes.

I have to confess that I missed many classes during my college years. My father's company supported paying for college, so I didn't have to work for my tuition. For me, dancing and performing were more important than going to class. It's shameful, and I feel sorry and apologize to my parents now. But I don't regret having considered other things more important than studying, and I feel that I won't make the same mistakes during the rest of my life.

So I earned money by marketing insurance during my senior year in college, and paid for and learned what I wanted to learn with that money. When I started earning and listening to expensive lectures paid with my own money, I started studying seriously and take action. I also got to ask the most questions at the lectures to learn more and more.

I searched for and took all the classes I needed to survive in society when I started out as a freelancer, not as a permanent worker who has a steady income. My attitude has changed since those early college years when my father's company paid for my education.

I don't feel inclined to accept that money can control a person's value judgment, but I can't help but admit it, due to the behavior and belief changes I've experienced in doing business. I went to a free lecture given by a famous person as well as a paid one. The content of the lectures was not very different. But in the paid lecture, more relatively enthusiastic people attended, asked the teachers questions, and received good interaction. There were more people who wanted to interact with the lecturer as well. Since then, I've seen a lot of cases where attendees establish a good relationship with their instructor. Of course, they learn and master the skills and knowledge faster than others.

The same goes for my seminars. In paid classes, students write down their questions, actively ask questions in the middle of the class, and after the discussion, try to resolve what they were curious about. This gives them a fortune worth dozens of times the money they paid for a class. If they try to solve problems alone, it might take a month or more, but from those seminars, they could cut down the time significantly.

Eighty years ago, fur clothing was sold at a store called Hwashin Department Store in Korea. The store owner had difficulties as the fur clothing wasn't selling well. What choices did the owner have in this situation? Did they offer a big discount event at the cost of their losses? No. The owner raised the price of fur 10 times. What do you think happened? All the clothes that hadn't sold over 10 days sold in a single day.

This is an example of how a product sets the price, but the price can also create value. Just imagine, how would you feel if a product you thought was a luxury item was set at a price cheaper than you thought it should be valued at? How do people respond? "Isn't this fake?" You would start to wonder. People also choose to buy luxury goods at a higher price without any suspicion.

What do you think? We must acknowledge that we're placing value on the product with price without realizing it. In particular, those who have to make money should insist on the proper price, not just a cheap price, to ensure the value of the product to the customer. You shouldn't offer a product at a poorly conceived discount or free of charge, because doing this might also lead to a discount of its value and a loss of good perception of the product as well.

It's only when the founder receives the proper payment that the quality of the goods and services are made better. Only then will the founder gain trust from customers as the founder's love for his or her own product will be reflected in the product. And it will increase sales as clients feel this value. The founder should continue to improve the product with conviction. They start by feeling the value beyond the price they set themselves. That feeling is the only way to excel at sales.

If the founder talks about the price of their product with anxiety or an awkward smile, customers are estranged. When sellers demand a fair price and as sales take place, the valuable goods add value to the customers.

When talking about a low price, the founder cannot expect his goods and services to become more valuable and they're only creating a loss. This is a fatal mistake. However, many startups still don't have the proper price set for their products and easily make this mistake. Of course, if you're a founder of a charity business who already has enough money, or if you're making a lot of money from other projects, I won't stop you. However, it's worth remembering that even so, poor pricing can deprive the customer of the opportunity to feel the true value of the product.

Finally, I'll tell you a funny anecdote that shocked me. It wasn't long after Butterfly Investment started. I was at the peak of efforts to sell more 1,100-dollar membership programs. Depending on the condition of the day, sales results had ups and downs.

Then I happened to meet a man who had a favorable view of our company's services. We exchanged greetings and asked after each other. He said he had been participating in a 10,000-dollar membership program from another institution. I was a little confused, but I asked carefully how he came to choose a service that was 10 times more expensive than our own. I received a shocking answer, and I would have regretted for the rest of my life if I hadn't asked and learned from the answer.

He told me the following. He had wanted to take the 1,000-dollar program, which is based on the spirit of Butterfly Investment, and was so valuable that it was worth taking. But then he paid for the 10,000-dollar program because he wondered how good it would be if it was 10 times more expensive than ours. Of course, he was satisfied with the service and was making lots of profits after the program. But after that, I met other people who told me the same story. Through these experiences, I believe our program is worth more than 100 million won ($100,000) for the services the company provides. And it will automatically sell in the multitudinous online markets without any discounts for five years.

3. If you make it good and sell it cheap, you'll go bankrupt.

This is one of the biggest mistakes people make when they step into the manufacturing industry from the standpoint of the consumer. It's a declaration of good quality and a big bargain.

At first glance, it seems obvious. And I guess the entrepreneurs heard somewhere that doing this will satisfy their clients and make their business succeed. In reality, however, we should not use this method recklessly until we experience what kind of mechanism works.

In particular, if you make up your mind at the beginning of your career, you'll be able to taste the bitter taste of a business startup. In fact, it's common to succeed in making a comeback when many of the failed founders didn't initially recognize their problems related to this issue. It's a concept that counts.

Some readers might ask, "Then shouldn't I make quality goods and sell them at a bargain?" That's not what I want to say here. There are certainly people who do business with good quality products at low prices. In the long run, the number of people receiving benefits increases as such business increases.

Usually, such entrepreneurs have the innovative cost-reduction tips they gained from starting businesses and surviving a long time rather than achieving these missions from the beginning. I'm writing this chapter to convey my advice and concern that if a startup founder runs the business this way, it's bound to collapse soon.

Making good quality products and selling them at a low price are both things to do if the company is to stay afloat. First, be honest with yourself. How many of you have a problem selling quality goods at a low price while not paying your employees a decent monthly paycheck, and while losing money to cover your family's living expenses? Is this the life of the founder you want to be? Or is it the life of the founder looking for urgent money? Did you choose this risky business startup to be recognized as *a clean business that has a great spirit of sacrifice, is able to serve, and is less greedy?*

You have to answer this very honestly. It's imperative that you survive in the real world in order to enjoy a truly carefree happiness and achieve your dreams. Before you decide to start a business, you might be sensitive to expensive goods throughout your life. Even though you didn't know about the profit structure, you may have felt displeased when others felt like they were making a high-profit margin. So you may have vowed not to do so and jumped into the startup front.

I fully understand that. However, if you become a provider and live your life in the real world, you'll face a reality that's different from that in the consumers' minds. You'll be lucky to sell a large number of low-value products and will feel your mind expand as you experience wonderful magic every month when you don't have any money at all. Making good quality and selling cheap is possible when the founder can maintain the business at a loss. Usually, it takes investment and loans to extend the period during which the business is held for a short time.

However, it will easily collapse further if it can't compete with the big company that is trying to dominate the market with more money and is able to attract investments. The more a founder competes, the more they are determined to win, and the more talented they are, the more difficult it is for them to endure. If you don't want to compete on the price, and if you don't want to sell it at a loss, you must first make it good and start with getting the proper price.

Obviously, it then takes more effort to find and create clients. However, it's much better to have a handful of cost-conscious customers if the quality is guaranteed than to have more price-conscious ones.

There are basic costs involved in making the quality better. It takes time and money to produce high-quality products unless you have innovative technologies that competitors don't. In fact, it's a big mistake to expect a large number of people to buy a product at a low price because almost all businesses try to sell at a bargain price. Even though the products are cheaper, you have to spend the money to do keyword marketing, blog marketing, and Facebook marketing.

Since there are no sales and no revenue, you have to pay the costs again with the money you already have. It's also common to pay marketing expenses without limit, and then the costs become higher than what you earn. Making money from marketing won't make your surplus funds. Although it's important for a startup to make the sales they target, they should pay particular attention to cost management. Otherwise, they'll find out much later that when they filled it with water, it was a broken vessel. They lose all the money previously earned and have regret.

At this point, I'd like to introduce a book that's impressed me, *Eighty Percent of Customers Buy Even If It Is Expensive* by Tatsuo Muramatsu. Eighty percent of the customers are not fools. If you make good quality products, set margins high enough to keep the business going, and deliver the value of the products, there are many customers who are sure to recognize them. So rather than talking about 80 percent of dumb customers, this book talks about high-quality customers.

Don't you think that if the price is low, the fact that the customer buys unconditionally is more like a judgment that lowers the value of the customer? Butterfly Investment's business ideas and products from cooperating companies are often pricey. Because they're expensive, the entrepreneurs can mobilize all of the ways they can deliver their products, create the content, with the founder's spirit, and grow platforms to make sure their business is being promoted.

They're making progress in this process by pondering and working with Butterfly Investment. If you only want to win at a low price, you must think about things you don't have to do. We can't win the favor of our clients unless we have a philosophy that's different from the ones that require cheap prices to win.

That's why the founders of each company are more likely to develop unique stories of their products, to continue producing relevant content in their daily lives, and to sell their products proudly. Again, nothing is more dangerous than starting with the idea that if you make a good product and sell it at a low price, you can just hope that sales will become better someday.

Initially, it will look like more customers may be interested in the product because it's cheap. Many customers may actually buy it because it's cheap. However, it will increase costs and require more staff. Usually, a founder will go through a vicious cycle during which they can't even cover labor costs with the margin they earn from cheaper goods.

This is not only about the deficit. A startup with limited resources is too busy dealing with a large number of customers, developing products, innovating, and expanding the business. As labor costs are so high, it's difficult to keep a person you like next to you. When people are hired on the basis of money, the founder becomes more stressed due to problems with human resources when staff quit.

It's impractical to expect staff to stay affectionate with a high volume of work, but small or delayed paychecks. Assuming the product is made with good quality and sold cheaply, it's hard to find any component at any point that will keep the business going.

A founder would have started the business with good intentions when they announced they would start a business under such a concept. But if they had more work, and no more money left to work, and if they felt stressed out about human resources problems, it would be easy for them to think there's no justice in the world. Negative thoughts then dominate the business. The founder loses interest in the business, thinks about tricks, and even tries to cheat the clients. Business can't be successful.

Surprisingly, the idea behind this vicious cycle is that it makes quality better, making it less expensive. You should always be able to look at the other side of the coin. I wouldn't tell anyone who still has a problem selling high-priced goods to sell to someone who doesn't like the product. But I would like to say you should get what you pay for.

I would like to say that we shouldn't start with unrealistic pricing methods that include only the price of raw materials in the cost. Include all costs that could be necessary to keep the business going. In addition to incorporating unforeseen costs, you should identify and reflect in the pricing the minimum elements to sustain the project, such as labor costs, electricity bills, service costs, and so on.

It's not impossible to offer a good quality product at a low price. But if you start like that, you'll never get there. It may sound cold, but there's no ideal starting place where anyone can succeed if they start only with good faith. If someone is willing to start a business with good faith without considering their survival, I tell them not to start it. I sincerely hope and pray that you will start a business, thrive, and deliver the good faith you want to convey to the world.

4. Three ways to build trust initially for pre-sales.

There's a saying "Distrust doubles transaction costs." The most difficult part about a prospective entrepreneur trying to get a lead is distrust from his friends and family. In fact, this can be different from person to person. When it comes to starting a business, few people deserve full support, but sometimes, people don't get support. Those who have gained support from acquaintances while taking this path that hasn't been easy for others have fewer deterrents in the preparation process for pre-sales. Basically, the trust they have built in people around them is unique. And because they're the ones who have made efforts to discover their own strengths in order to build such trust, they share confidence and humility in their speech and manner.

If you've never established trust, enough to be recognized while challenging a different method in the past, you'll be hurt by public distrust while attempting pre-sales. In that case, you can look back on your past and look back on your attitude and tone. There was little chance for us to learn what language and attitude we should have in order to have the most confidence as well as to be sympathetic. If you hadn't tried to sell to customers because you didn't know how to start a zero-base startup and how to conduct pre-sales, you wouldn't have had a chance to feel uncomfortable.

The theme to be discussed in this chapter are the words, attitudes and facial expressions of the founder, which are the most influential in building new trust with the client.

However, if you want to start a business and overcome trial and error quickly and make a lot of money, you should pay careful attention to these areas. That's because these efforts help to increase trust and lower transaction costs. As the rest of the book deals with this, in this chapter I'll reveal one of the ways to build trust.

First, don't say that your services and products cover everything the customer wants.

More specifically, you might want to deliberately mention areas you can't cover. Traditionally, entrepreneurs promote their services to solve more problems and help more people. People think doing this will make them more professional and make more money. However, it's not like that at all. For example, let's say there are two Chinese restaurants in front of you. One says, "This restaurant is delicious with jajangmyeon, jjambbong, and sweet and sour pork!" And the other says, "Our jjambbong is best of the world! Eat jajangmyeon at another restaurant!' If you really want to eat jjambbong, which one would you choose between the two? Which slogan do you think is more straightforward and reliable? Of course, it's the second one.

Why is that? Because the second one said that they can't do well with both, and they are honest. It's better not to suggest things that you don't excel at. When you say an item falls short of perfection, you give customers more trust. You also give customers reasonable expectations. Also, the founder admits the shortcoming, so customers won't respond negatively to that point.

Ironically, I was able to engage with investors several times while running Butterfly Investment, which says, "Don't get investments and loans." I also had a proposal to build up a business to help me receive some investments. But I didn't take the investments. I only pledged to make Butterfly Investment more aware of the venture as professionally focused on zero-base startups.

That's why I always emphasize that Butterfly Investment never tells you anything about getting a loan or investments. Money doesn't spoil our color. The keyword "zero-base startup" became attached to Butterfly Investment like a magnet. A startup business that has yet to develop a proper prototype, with a founder who has yet to be significantly affected by customers' compliments, cannot say that it can cover everything. Rather, doing that would make customers lose their trust and confidence in this company. Say you can't do what you can't do. And tell your client that your product doesn't cover 100 percent. At that moment, credibility will soar.

Second, tell clients a concrete and rigid number.

Actually, this is something I care a lot about, but it's not easy for me either. The entrepreneurs are easily tempted to keep up with their business and to show their performance by using vague numbers, skillfully avoiding lies, and maximizing performance. For example, they want to say that the group's monthly sales are a couple of million, even if they were just one million. Instead, for example, I would like to say that I've cofounded dozens of companies even if I've cofounded just 20. This pattern is also in line with saying, "I can't cover everything. "

Anyway, the exaggerated information gives unreasonable expectations to customers. If the number is mentioned in a few vague words, customers feel uncomfortable and build distrust unconsciously. At the beginning of the project, there's not much to be said for numbers. However, there are still some numbers that can appeal. It can be appealing if the entrepreneur has made a lot of their own content, especially if they spend time at the beginning of the business and make a lot of content and stories.

The figures that take a long time to acquire continue to build. I had a personal YouTube channel before, but once I made a zero-base startup channel, I created many videos at a fast pace. Within a year, I produced and uploaded about 200 videos. This is what numbers can build to through hard work.

There's something else that can make numbers appealing only with time. I've been hosting a business-idea forum every month and have been producing and sharing business-idea documents for 200 weeks. I've been teaching for 200 weeks. If you don't have proven numbers, don't hide behind vague numbers. You'll see there are numbers that give you records and credibility, and trust that time creates. It's better to create large numbers that can appeal through effort and deliver confidence to customers.

Third, deliver the real story. I said that a startup founder selling products should have affection for their products. I keep emphasizing that I needed to start my own business because I discovered why I had to do it, and I liked it, not because others told me that it would go well. Even if you don't like it now, you need to study what you want to know for a long time, educate yourself, and grow your own business. Creating a business item brings one's own life to the field.

A company that wanted to carry out a P2P (peer to peer) lending business continuously appeared and disappeared. News of investments was also heard frequently. I didn't invest money but if I chose one of those companies, I'd hear how much the founder's life was projected into it.

For example, founder A came and said, "Isn't financial technology the trend? We started our business because we had a good market and a good view." On the other hand, founder B came to me and said, "I tried to get a loan while I was running my own business, but I couldn't get a loan. I looked for everything I could do to get a loan, and I ended up starting a business with it." And, of course, I would invest in B.

It's hard to convey confidence just by providing customers with a book-like guide or information from internet research. The real story should be told. The credibility of a business increases when you include the story of an actual business episode, the story of a customer case changed by the service, the story of a happy customer, and the story of a creator.

I also recommend that the founders I coach establish a lecture plan based on their true story. This is why it's necessary to manage a small number of customers in the early stage of the project while making efforts to increase the level of satisfaction. It's difficult to draw reviews and stories from customers who are satisfied while managing multiple customers at one time.

Proceed with sales based on actual experiences. It will be your turn as a humble but reliable entrepreneur.

I'd like to mention as a bonus one more way that the startup owner builds trust. For those of you who thought it had ended in three things, the bonus is deliberately offered as if it were good news. A bonus tip has to do with the trust that comes from just holding on. I mentioned a little bit about the record of numbers made over time. Be connected to that part. Trust comes when a person thought likely to quit their business soon instead doesn't quit and continues to develop it. This dramatic reversal brings trust and credibility. People think they can't stand it any longer, but if they hold on, they'll be surprised and gain trust. There's trust that comes from continuing to work.

There's nothing more reliable than longevity and persistence. As long as you are about to start your business, take advantage of the three previous points of know-how, and one day you'll receive meaningful trust. Once you do, hold on to it and build trust, and you'll eventually see the way.

5. After all, sales are the first priority for all businesses.

"Business models that come from competition."

"Business models that maximize value to specific customer groups."

"Business models that turn everyday life into money."

I've written about 150 business ideas. The documents are about 10 pages and contain business background information and market need, target customers, advance strategies, obstacles, and missions. These documents are being shared with membership customers.

Among them are several documents aimed at starting a physical store. These documents help you start sales of your products with the goal of starting a store safely in the long run. One of the idea documents is the shopless cafe. It's a business that delivers only americanos and lattes from Starbucks, Ediya, The Coffee Bean and Tea Leaf and other famous cafes. These cafes are gathered within a certain radius of a busy office. The price of each americano and latte is slightly different, and the price is printed on shopless Cafe's flyer and business card.

It's a business that delivers cafe menu items to customers for 1,000 to 2,000 won ($1 to $2) in delivery fees if they order after looking at a flyer. The founder stays at any cafe that day and delivers the order through Kakao Talk or other messengers. Delivery time is quick because orders are placed at an office near the cafe.

The main target is people who don't want to line up for drinks, important guests in the office who can't be served with instant coffee, and people who can't run errands for employees. Most of the time customers go to buy coffee themselves because they don't want to pay for delivery, but I'm sure some people would like to have their coffee delivered.

How much money could you make in this way? It depends on your efforts, but you might not earn much in the beginning. However, you could experience by trial and error how to start a cafe delivery business without having to spend a lot of money. You could try different ideas safely to sell more. Then, the flyer develops and becomes more sophisticated.

You should wear a nice suit to make deliveries, deliver coffee in a polite manner, and manner, and tell the customer to have a happy day. You can think of all this as practice in case you start your own cafe one day. There are no expenses anyway.

You'll impress customers if you take note of special situations and remember specifics from conversations with them, and mention these details when you see the customers again. All of this is what you can do when you actually start your own cafe. You can earn money before you open a cafe and learn these skills without risk.

You'll turn into a salespreneur who makes sales first, pays expense later, and makes profits. In this way, some customers even give tips every time they order the coffee delivery. Some of those customers will recommend the owner of the cafe, which can eventually lead you to take over the management of more cafes.

In fact, there are people who run one cafe well and share their profits by taking their know-how to run another cafe. If you have the know-how to sell well and get regular customers, you can continue to expand the number of cafes as a zero-base startup. We're not talking about staying with a plausible idea, but about a case that exists in reality.

If you've secured regular customers through delivery, it will be easier to operate your own cafe. If you have a large number of customers, you can guarantee a certain monthly profit. If you secure regular customers through good sales, you can operate the cafe yourself or negotiate with the owner of the existing cafe and operate it in the form of revenue distribution.

The choice to scale up should be made after sales training and after generating more than a certain amount of revenue without relying on capital. This will reduce the chances of failure and allow the founder to survive longer and grow again. If the company can't withstand the phase of sales training, it's right to give up the desire to expand the business. This is because even if the founder borrows money and expands, they'll face the same problem and won't make profits.

Cho Jung-il—who creates LEGO art and is the CEO of Brick Factory—had a dream to own his own gallery. However, it's not easy trying to create a gallery from scratch, which is costly in the beginning and difficult to recover costs from. So now, he's doing sales training through the idea of a cafe gallery, which is among the documents I made. He's affiliated with a cafe where he'll be able to show his art. The art pieces will hang in the affiliated cafe, and the artist proposes to divide the profits with the cafe if the pieces are sold.

With the simple sale of coffee, the cafe can't make a big profit. The agony of cafe owners is that they can't change the interior often either. Artists are good at making things, but they have a hard time selling them. Establishing pricing, making contracts, negotiating, and talking about money are uncomfortable subjects. Artists are the brightest when they make their own art, but only if their work continues to sell.

Based on an idea document that solves problems on both sides, CEO Cho Jung-il will work with cafes and artists. It's a proposal to make more profit to those who are self-employed. There's no reason to refuse taking advantage of the space that already exists to create opportunities for profitability without an additional workforce.

In this way, Cho will be able to consult on the art of painting the cafe and expand the business without paying any expenses in partnership with artists.

As he meets various cafe owners and learns from their trials and errors and know-how, he's working with them and consulting with them on a profit model. In addition, he's interacting with creative artists and helping them make profits.

Imagine opening your own gallery cafe after this process. You could open it by taking advantage of know-how and networking and making profits. Don't be under the impression that a good service and marketing strategy will bring in many customers and boost sales from the start.

If you go through sales training in advance, you can feel relieved, as well as understand how difficult it is to run a cafe. You'll find that it's necessary to practice smiling and saying hello aloud.

Cho had never imagined he could meet the cafe owners and propose a profit model. But now he's meeting with cafe owners, listening to their stories, making suggestions, and achieving a broader perspective.

Without this process, if people start a store with money, they naturally go through a process of closing business after worrying about the money. I continue to witness people undergoing this sad process.

I can come up with the idea of starting a new business for those people. It's possible because Choi is the first person to do so, and he kept training me.

If a client who's trying to change their business model after months of worry comes to me, I'm confident that I can suggest new ideas to solve the problems in less than an hour. I wasn't that sort of person before, but I became that person as I'd been doing the same tasks almost every day for years. It would be strange if I hadn't been this person for five years, with weekly lectures and solutions to a variety of business problems. There is no problem that can't be solved, and the key to the solution lies in the client's own mind.

If I had opened the office from the start and said I would coach while having that expense, I wouldn't have been able to get to this stage. I would have been impatient and over-coached because of ongoing costs. To cover the costs, I would have gone around getting loans and investments. Sales may have been pushed back.

I also did sales first and studied hard to reward the customers who trusted me with my weaknesses. Fortunately, I made a lot of money, so I had more time to study first and go through more trial and error, and based on that, I could train salespreneurs. As a man who had been at the bottom for a long time, I couldn't lose my modesty. It was possible for me to benefit from the meditation I practiced to endure on the ground and to feel what it was like to communicate with the world at that stage.

I didn't meet customers with the intention of getting answers right away. I learned that it was my job to respond purely to their voices, to feel empathy, and to drive their potential. I felt that I had accumulated some wisdom I had gained from countless exchanges with my teachers. What I learned emerged from the moment I was immersed, and it resonated with my customers.

Currently, I'm using a coworking office in Seoul called CityCube, provided by Lee Seung-hwan, CEO of CityCube, a Butterfly Investment membership client. Profitability also pays for these spaces, but there's no problem returning to a state free of space at any time. If a self-employed person becomes a sales agent who can sell themselves well, they don't have to worry if they want to get rid of the store. The owner of the cafe, who has created regular customers, can go to other cafes, continue managing, and find other cafes to join. The CEO of the cafe gallery can make money by making a profit model at other cafes even if they close their own.

Those who think about their own business must also build salespreneurship and start a business afterwards. That way, they can survive and earn money without depending on any physical space such as cafes or offices. Or, even if a store is opened, salespreneurship can secure stable profits to run a business.

6. The secret "4 Ps" to make your customer buy.

How can you make your products appealing to lead to sales?

There are several sales marketing classes and different methods to refer to. However, if a salesperson understands when they listen but they can't execute it, then it's of no use to learn so many methods. It's more important to remember and execute those sales tricks you have learned to use.

For instance, people study a lot and read books for the purpose of writing well. This way, they can recognize which sentences are good and which are bad. But if they don't actually write, they'll never learn how to write. Rather, just thinking about a variety of advice is a hindrance to writing.

So when I write, I write comfortably and write everything I want first. Then I simply delete the words I see as "hostile." I delete redundant words from the text. You can use these easy-to-remember tips immediately to make them your own skills.

It's also easy to remember and use the 4 Ps I'm about to explain. If you use the 4 Ps to explain a certain product to a customer, create a sales phrase, post a sales statement, and make a presentation, you'll create a strong sales effect.

Promise

After you read the secret 4 Ps to make your customer buy, you'll have strong sales power. Part one of the promise is one of the most used in my daily life. At the beginning of the sales seminar, I show a summary of the benefits of the seminar.

It's been a lecture for more than three years now, "Startup! Sales Is First," which also speaks of its benefits.

1. The secret of the long-running business: pre-sales.

2. How to do business with what you like and what you want to learn.

3. An approach to establishing expensive prices.

4. A sales approach to open the customer's mind.

I say in the beginning that participants or students of this seminar will learn the four tips above. This is the promise. This makes students expect to gain benefits from the class, and it makes them focus well during the lecture. Without such guides or promises, the students will interpret the lecture in their own way and won't concentrate on it. Even in the sales situation, it's good to have such a promise at the beginning.

When you have a meeting to sell insurance, you can say, "From today's meeting, you'll certainly know if you have insurance you don't need." This makes your clients concentrate and focus more on what you say.

There's one case in which the promise can be applied even more. It's a video clip. Not only large companies but also startups are using an explosive number of video advertisements these days.

According to a 2016 South Korean advertising cost analysis conducted by Cheil Wordwide, the growth rate of mobile video ads has already overtaken the search ad. Google and Facebook are also competing with YouTube's and Facebook Watch's video platforms, and they're competing with each other to sell video advertisements, making video content more powerful.

There are countless video clips promoting products, and they're ready to play. In this case, the promise strategy helps to increase concentration level on video clips. The promise makes reference to what can be obtained from the image within the first five seconds of the image.

Or, you can have a strong comment at the beginning that makes people look forward to the latter part. If the first five seconds don't produce something that catches the customer's attention with the promise, the rest of the video becomes a useless video no matter whether it is one minute or 10 minutes long. People lose their attention without the promise in the beginning. Therefore, the promise in the beginning, plays an important role.

Picture

What is it that beats reason? Is it a feeling? When you fall in love, you lose your reason. It's easy to think you've lost your mind when you make a choice that makes your heart beat. The feeling is strong. Reasonably persuasive sales are, therefore, the dumbest way to sell.

Unless the salesperson and customer agree rationally and understand each other, it's hard to appeal. If you talk rationally and make any mistakes, it's inevitable that you'll engage in an argument with the client.

That's why salespeople tell us to sell with storytelling. It's a way to talk about the service with ease and to explain the service to clients. People respond to stories with their emotions. When the benefits of a product are delivered through a popular story, the customer feels happier.

If a salesperson sells water purifiers, and they ramble about the mineral content of the water, expandable filters, and descriptions of the countries where the products are produced, a customer could quickly close their ears. But a customer would respond differently if the salesperson said, "After drinking water from the water purifier, my immune system improved. I've recommended this water purifier to many people, and they've seen improvements after drinking the water, so I moved forward and started a business." If you've proven this statement to be true and have a customer who's concerned about their own immune system, they'll listen carefully to the story.

Remember that the customer's chest responds when he or she is able to visualize a story. It's not easy to draw a picture for a client with a rational explanation. However, many people still list numerical information as they conduct sales, and put the hard data before the customer's eyes. Of course, the customer is confused, and even if the customer had good feelings, they now feel rather reluctant.

The founder should consider whether to describe the product with examples and stories as if drawing a picture in the mind of the customer.

Proof

Earlier in the promise section, I mentioned this: "After you read the secret 4 Ps to make your customer buy, you'll have strong sales power." And in that, I made the promise about the benefits of this book. The customer will pay attention from start to end because of initial expectations—the promise—of the future benefits.

What do you think? If you've been reading this book, you know I've proved the effects of the promise. The proof is actually showing. Nothing is so powerful as when it's actually displayed.

For instance, to explain how strong a new smartphone is, it's better to display this rather than to tell how hard it was dropped in certain lab tests. Simply drop the phone in front of clients and show them.

Butterfly Investment is responsible for spreading the way in which business is done in the real world without capital and sets up companies only that way. We guide business startups through the process to discard consumer perspectives completely.

We also encourage startups to choose items that are out of competition and to create a new monopoly market. Business models should be refined so that business can proceed without physical offices. They can do business online. We require businesses to benchmark Butterfly Investment as these businesses develop their own social network sites to build trust online.

However, it's not enough to explain the concepts. It's more efficient to show the cases of startups that were created with Butterfly Investment as examples. Or you can show the company websites, lectures, and books published by startup owners from Butterfly Investment.

At the beginning of the project there's no foundation, but if you follow Butterfly Investment's guidance and directly show the content it helps you provide, you won't need to create long explanations.

Storytelling provides a picture of the product that the customer can imagine, while proof eliminates any doubt from the customer. Beyond your telling the story of an improved immune system after drinking water from water purifier, the proof is what makes customers drink the water and feel better.

Pitch

A popular startup term that's commonly used is *pitching*. To explain your item to an investor or prospective customer is called *pitching*. The word *pitch* originated from baseball: The *pitcher* throws the ball. People use the word *pitch* to explain to the customer to *catch* the product well.

Even if you keep the first 3 Ps in mind, the result won't be produced if you don't make the last pitch. I emphasize repetitive pitches to those who are preparing to start a business. Pitch is the sales. Pitch becomes increasingly difficult if you don't get used to it sooner.

It's good to get used to pitching when you're initially enthusiastic. In particular, if entrepreneurs practice pitch with the 3 Ps in mind first, customers will respond favorably and have less resistance to sales.

There's an important point to make about the pitch. Your child can't catch a ball well at first if you throw a big, heavy ball. Even if you throw several balls at once, it's hard to catch one. This means that you should consider giving the customer a minimal selection plan to avoid disruption while excluding the factors that prevent them from making the sales decision.

For instance, suppose you want to set up a direct payment system at a site where customers can register for lectures easily. However, if the procedure to sign up for the site is complex, and the payment process is complicated, the customer will no longer be willing to pay. As the provider conducts the payment process, it's necessary to identify the factors that are inconvenient for the customer and are preventing payment, and to find alternatives.

Amazon's one-click payment system is a good example of a one-step process that captures the customer easily. Requesting more than one action at a time makes it difficult to capture the customer. And giving customers a chance to compare various options makes them more annoyed.

The system should convey a key message that's easily recognizable by the customer and makes them capable of taking immediate action. When someone asks me, "What advice can Taesoon Shin give to the founder who is afraid of sales?" If I reply, "You can see my YouTube videos, come to my offline lectures, visit my homepage, or visit my online community," then there's no energy from each action and no impact. However, if I said, "Let's go ahead and see my video clip 'How to Start Your Business' first," I take away the customer's pain. And they catch a pitch that works because it's one action.

Keep in mind the 4 Ps I mentioned and apply them to sales, and you'll gain strong sales power.

7. Sales know-how: Draw a picture inside the customer's mind.

There was a time in the past when it was popular for a dialect to be a used as a theme at Gag Concert, which was a famous comedy show in Korea. It's not uncommon to use a word as a comedy subject in a situation where someone has trouble communicating while using different regional dialects. Even though it's Korean, the usage and intonation of the words vary depending on the region, and because of that, the meanings are completely changed.

If you're a salesperson, you should take extra care not to cause misunderstanding when delivering your product. Language is a good way to communicate, but it can also be a dangerous tool that causes fatal misunderstandings and breaks communication.

People who often use Chinese characters and use more difficult terms think they look like experts. And the so-called experts who communicate this way don't feel bad about it. Rather, they're satisfied they've presented their image well as an expert.

But if you stick to that image, the opportunity to generate revenue from sales is rather low. I think it's a real expert who knows difficult terms but can explain them easily to children without using them.

It's important to be professional with the products you sell. For sales to occur, however, you should be able to convey information easily to people who don't know the goods at all. Therefore, it's one thing to think about studying long enough, or to have a lot of professional knowledge, and quite another to be good at sales.

In fact, experts who studied hard at the start of their business enjoyed a sense of superiority in front of customers, who were locked into their knowledge and knew only the terms they knew. In such cases, customers are less likely to feel the value of the product and rather more likely to feel uncomfortable. Obviously, it's difficult for sales to take place.

If sales don't occur, experts blame the customer's ignorance. The expert is too absorbed in intellectual vanity to reflect on their own limitation. If you stick to your limitation, you'll only experience the worst selling, during which the more you try, the more inconvenient the customer becomes.

You can only change if you meet a world you haven't seen before. There are some great selling experts who combine knowledge with intuition. You have to meet such a master, listen to their advice, and not feel shy about recognizing your own limitations. Or you'll only feel the need to change if you have to go to the bottom several times because you haven't been able to make sales for a long time.

If you have a lot of knowledge about the product but can't get the product across a young child, it's just half knowledge.

Rich knowledge shines when it comes to the wisdom of conveying that knowledge. I would describe this wisdom as the ability to go inside and outside the box. Seeing a box in a box is one thing, and seeing a box outside of a box is quite another.

If the person in the box hears the description of the outside of the box, it makes no sense to tell the story of the box they're looking at. It's embarrassing when a customer says they don't understand the box when you're working hard to explain it. Looking at the same box inside and outside is a completely different experience.

The seller must be able to explain what's in and out of the box. Customers who can only see inside the box need to hear a description they understand so they can see outside the box.

Otherwise, even if the seller and customer communicate for a long time on the same topic, they have very different pictures, conflicting opinions, and confusion in their minds. Those who sell benefit from being more sensitive.

There's a game that four or five celebrities sometimes play on entertainment programs. It's a game about listening to a word from the producers and acting it out to explain the word at the same time. And they all score points if they do the same thing. I've never seen this game played the same way twice.

Simple words for exercise—like baseball, basketball, and swimming—and animals—like cats and dogs—are given, but every player in the game expresses them with different motions.

This is because even if you hear the same word, in your mind it brings different images. Even more so, this happens with words related to unfamiliar products. What about professional words you don't write often? A businessperson who knows the goods well and a customer who has no information at all can only paint an image with the words they use.

Easier words are more likely to create shared images. Using specific words rather than abstract words makes it simpler for customers to create images in their minds. Even if the customer uses words related to color and temperature, it's easy for the customer to recall images vividly. It's better to use an expression that stimulates the senses rather than to list facts.

Now, let's think about the way customers are satisfied with their products. Has this occurred to you? Now, let's think about the way our customers are satisfied with their products and smile when they use them.

You will feel better when you describe the situation more specifically and use words that touch the five senses. In addition, when selling products, the customer must recall the image of the product without any obstacles to making the purchase.

Only when you use difficult words and abstract words can you recognize yourself as an expert and get rid of the illusion that the customer will pay for the product. It's an unfulfilling approach to increasing sales. Highlight it again. To sell well, you need to consciously choose easy words and choose words that will stimulate the senses.

The mission of this chapter is to explain to a five-year-old child the products and services you want to sell. Obviously, this will be different from the comments and phrases traditionally used in the minds of prospective clients. This will be filled with words that are much easier to integrate into everyday life. You'll also begin to see the terms and assumptions you used, assuming you already knew them.

In fact, this is what I consider most important in writing each book. I'm a person who redefines the meaning of zero-base startup and continues to talk about things that aren't common knowledge. The theme itself is unfamiliar. However, I thought it was foolish to address these experiences with terms I alone understand.

I've put a lot of effort into writing the first draft, but I've spent twice as much time making it easier to understand. Of course, it was the same for my second book, and I did it while writing this book.

You have to write easy words and use words related to the five senses to be applauded by readers. Sales are no different. From now on, you should transform into a painter who paints images with colorful pictures in your mind.

8. It takes time for the customer's wallet to open.

It's not easy to get real support from people around you at the beginning of your startup business.

Most office workers will be told to keep their job and work hard. If you're a student, you'll be scolded for starting a business because you didn't get a job. Thus, although the early stage of business is full of passion, it's a time when people are easily swayed due to lack of support from family and friends.

They may even rule out friends who don't help them. They often don't want to see friends who talk negatively about the business and get angry with them. But before you talk about these things to your friends recklessly, step back and think about it all calmly again.

Wouldn't it be the same if you were in your friends' shoes? If things were reversed, you would have to say something similar to what your friends said to you. You'd think it's for their own good. It wouldn't be easy to expect someone who has never owned a business to be good at it at first. You'd really want to stop them, and inside you would think this.

"He'll be back in three months."

"She'll be tired in six months."

Of course, there are others who are likely to be doing well in business. Even at work and school, there are quite a few people who continue to host meetings or projects on what they want to do in the future. They're more likely to be supported when they leave their jobs and say they're doing something to start their own business. They've built trust and brand by continuously showing more than others around them.

If you didn't want to take any action to prepare yourself for starting a business, and then suddenly declare you'll start your own business just because you don't want to be employed or you hate your job, you can't expect support from people around you. This is also understandable if you change your mind.

If you start your own business this way, everybody will think like this: "Even if I help him in the early stages of the business, I might lose money, and if I buy a product, I might not be able to get the right kind of service for it because he might quit the business soon."

It should be expected that you won't be supported at first, as friends are concerned that they could lose their precious relationship with you in this vague situation. Only with this mindset can we deal with various mental failures we may experience in the beginning. If you start a business, thinking about the network around you will help you; you'll be hurt more deeply than you thought.

After listening to this, we can find an easy solution to the problem. A little less expectation and support from your friends and acquaintances are enough to keep the business going. And you can show them you're running the business longer than they expected. People tend to think that if they don't get their customers now, they will fail, but this is a mistake.

My co-founder Choi runs a lecture business through the company called School Monster. Now, a large number of CEOs of zero-base startups are also working as instructors there. In the past, when both Choi and I conducted the classes, I used to sell 1-million-won worth of lectures a day.

Did this lecture sell immediately when we announced it? I don't think so. I posted an introduction to the lecture every week for about two months. Payment didn't occur, and each week he tried to sell lectures online, continuing to change his weekly introduction and table of contents. It wasn't a difficult task to do every week since it didn't cost anything to revise and post the lecture introduction online.

Some people who post lectures are promoting them a few times only, but they're disappointed if no one registers soon. They rarely change the introduction, don't share the post links to more websites, and repeat them less often. But I don't do that. I knew there were many people watching the introduction page for the 1-million-won lecture out there. I kept doing this for about two months.

Observers might think that if we post it this way, and the customer doesn't pay, we'll definitely quit soon. But as time goes by, something interesting happens. More and more people start to watch these lecture advertisements, and they start to wonder what will be presented in the lecture and what will be updated next time.

As a month or two passes, the number of viewers on the page that introduces the lecture increases. This leads to projects beyond the expectations of those who thought the businessperson would soon quit. People are confused by the constant development of the lecture introduction pages through a longer period than they expected.

"Am I wrong? Are they really selling these products because they're confident? Don't they have any intention of quitting? Are they really going to continue?"

Thinking about this, someone who considers signing up for the lecture begins to question their hasty judgment. The number of people with questions increases. And with these questions, someone appears who pays with conviction after carefully examining the information to resolve his or her curiosity.

Other people who watched also build the courage to pay for it. When a customer crosses the point where their expectations are exceeded, they're surprised. The value they feel as a result of the surprise is larger and more provocative. Customers open their wallets at that point. The amount of time it takes for a customer to open their wallet is in proportion to the time you devoted to giving them the surprise as a present.

So, what kind of business should we choose in order to get a business that offers more than expected? It's also necessary for the founder to be able to enjoy the items and to choose items closely associated with their daily life. When it's a business item that brings about its own growth and solves problems, it's likely to endure beyond the expectations of its clients. Business items that don't meet these criteria will never last long.

It's difficult to convey the sincerity of the founder when they have a business item that will change whenever the founder can't afford it. Customers open their wallets with no worries when the founder stays in business beyond the customer's expectations, continues to develop business items, and shows pleasure in business.

The customer is smart. Customers are reluctant to waste their money and affection on projects that are clearly marked by the founder's pursuit of money, projects that are entirely devoid of the founder's enjoyment, and projects that are unlikely to have longevity.

9. Five things to keep in mind for startup companies not to fail.

"My business item isn't good. It won't work; it will fail."

No one would start their business with these thoughts. I think it's foolish to have a negative idea, even though I can't think of an item as a good thing. I'm a positive thinker and recommend to those who have their own business to start a positive mind-training program. Nevertheless, there's also danger in only believing in the illusion of a future as something fantastic, so this chapter introduces some guidelines that help you train your mind before starting a business.

First, you need to learn how to motivate yourself.

Just drinking alcohol and crying over the pain doesn't make you strong. On the contrary, this can backfire, hurting your health and causing others to avoid you. Though you tried to escape your problems in the past, you should start training to cope with difficulties differently from the moment you decide to start a business. For example, look for music that can cheer you up when hard times arrive. In my case, a strong beat of electronic music was the thing that cheered me up and encouraged me.

Also, you can find your own place where you feel most comfortable. In my case, it was a sauna. My co-founders also have their own separate spaces to give them comfort and strength. Some people gain power from the sea, some from the arboretum, and others from the art museum.

You can also find supporting videos. I was greatly comforted by watching videos of Professor Kim Chang-ok in Korea. You can also gain power with voices. These days, the themes of podcasts are so diverse that you can easily find content that is right for you if you look carefully. Those who are trying to start their own business can find the podcast "The Pirate's Startup Story" or Naver's audio clip "Pouring Oil on Zero-Base Startup" (all available in Korean only). These channels allow people to access the light and darkness of entrepreneurs at the same time.

As long as you plan to start a business, you'd better make such routines before you start it. After you start a business, your mind can break down easily, and troubles can drive you out of control and can consume all of your energy. When that happens, you should restore your condition quickly by using your own pre-developed motivation methods. With the help of these tools, startup owners can endure the hard times and grow day by day.

Second, try to live without money. Even if you have money, you should experience life without money.

It's a necessary practice for office workers who have a stable income to decide to start their own business. This is because without eliminating the fear of living without money, you can't come to the path of starting a business. If you spend $50 on average a day, you should reduce it to $30, or even $10 from there, or even down to $3 a day. In fact, I lived for a long time on only $2 to $3 a day when I started. I didn't have much money, and I wondered how I could survive in this extreme situation.

Surprisingly, in this extreme situation, I learned many things to survive. If I steeled myself and put a smile on my face, I could live on less money while pursuing what I wanted. If one fears not having enough money, it's easy to choose to return to your old job immediately after starting a business, or it's difficult to make the decision to quit your job.

The goal of living without money is this: You find that you can maintain your lifestyle with less than you thought, and you're free to do whatever you want. Let's not waste precious time in life without growth under the pretext of earning 100 dollars a day when we can live with less money than we expected.

Third, find a role model.

There's a saying: "Get on the shoulders of giants." I met good teachers, and I was a lucky rider on their shoulders. Many people are amazed at how I grew up with such crazy ideas and went into business at an early age. I think depending on which role model you meet; you can gain 50 years of wisdom in only 10 to 20 years.

When choosing role models, you shouldn't pick people who have already joined the ranks of complete success. Of course listening to them is a good idea, but there's a limit to being inspired by past stories when they aren't currently on the playing field. As long as they're playing in the field, they can be your role models.

Of course, there is something to be cautious about. Don't find a role model who's only been successful from start to end. The know-how of a person who knows how cold it feels when they were at the bottom is real. Don't make a role model of a person who's too busy to cut off their rivals, who says they are the only one who is good at what they do. That's a person who keeps making enemies, and they're full of anxiety in their heart. You may believe in them as a role model, and then that negative energy might spread to you someday.

Don't make a role model of someone who hides the fact that they were successful thanks to luck and the help of others. That person may take advantage of their luck and will soon lose it. People like this easily lose their original intentions, and when things don't work out, they often blame others. It's necessary to observe more of their daily life and not to judge them by their fancy cover.

Fourth, get used to working 10 hours a day.

After reading my first book—*I Work Only Four Hours a Week and Earn 10 Million Won a Week*—many people said that they wanted to live that way. However, there were people who mistakenly thought that the systems and branding I had described could be built in a short period of time without cost or labor. I spent close to $100,000 dollars to study various new things after I graduated from college and had no stable revenue for five years. I spent more than 10 hours a day creating content to build up an online and offline brand, and the money earned was reinvested and the process repeated.

Fortunately, I liked studying new things. I found that I could turn new things into money, so I studied hard happily. It takes a long time to produce tangible output. Through these times, my mind was strengthened, and I could build up tiny but significant details to contribute to the information I provide for others. Such invested time is the key to my developing new topics every week while I give different lectures.

Even if there were a way to do less work and make more money right now, I wouldn't choose that way. That's because I'm sure that such a way would not be under my control. Obviously, it would become a charade and a stress to go in that other direction. I feel comfortable and confident in earning money by making use of the content and brand that I have worked hard for, and am living a free life.

When you become a CEO, it's only in the distant future that you will only give orders, and that employees will do your job. Early in the business, new entrepreneurs who sell products through pre-sales grow themselves, develop products, and improve customer satisfaction themselves. If you don't make such efforts early because you received the money in advance, you'll become a swindler. It's the power of the pre-sales to create a situation in which it's imperative to work so hard early on.

Fifth, embrace sales.

The word of startups looks fancy and nice. You can choose paths that others don't choose often, find new ways out in the world, and make a lot of money in the future. But be careful not to become arrogant with the pride of starting a startup. A startup business itself isn't cool anymore. It might raise one's self-esteem to use words that sound good and feel cool, but I think it's rather poisonous.

Startup owners tend to stay away from sales. If you're an entrepreneur, you should come closer to sales. Sales should be brought closer to your daily life. Sales should be your closest task even though sometimes this hurts your pride and people misunderstand you. Otherwise, sales slip away in a second. I created various content and give lectures to inspire people to start their own business. But the key to all of that is sales.

I transform the word "sales" into many variations and guide the entrepreneur through. An entrepreneur might say, "I'm not right for sales." Or, "I'm going to think about sales as far as I can." If you say this, you'll never succeed even if you start a business. You should approach your business with the idea of learning your own sales style.

I was such a timid person, and I couldn't even ask for a favor. So it took me a long time to get used to sales. However, I sold products that I was told are crazy and established a process that automatically creates sales online. Most of my partners who started their business with Butterfly Investment were far from sales. But they learned how to become familiar with sales, and then became sales experts through training. At this stage, all content that entrepreneurs create becomes a powerful weapon with sales capabilities. There's no comparison between the content made by someone who doesn't know how to sell and the value of content made by someone who knows how to sell.

Few people really understand why Butterfly Investment emphasizes person-to-person sales to entrepreneurs and makes them go through that phase even if they are tired and embarrassed. The zero-base startup entrepreneurs who started their business with their sales through Butterfly Investment are growing rapidly. They use all tools at their best efficiency. All this is possible because sales are their priority.

10. Three things easily missed when presenting a sales seminar.

I began going to sales seminars when I was selling insurance. When I started selling insurance, I read one book a day and attended a seminar once a week to learn how to sell more. I felt the strength of sales seminars in the midst of such a study. However, I never dreamed of holding my own seminar that would gather potential customers even if I wrote my own blog. Then later, in 2010, I made my own websites and wrote articles there with WordPress, and I connected it with Facebook pages and attracted traffic. I also tried to make contact with potential end users. However, I felt that I couldn't convert traffic into sales without offline exchanges even though I appealed to potential customers through exposure to the web. Therefore, I started learning how to conduct an offline seminar to draw more sales.

In fact, speaking in front of strangers without fear was the most frightening task for me, but I overcame my fear by learning at sales seminars. I paid for classes, and as I learned, I was forced to speak in front of people and listen to the teachers' feedback.

There are a number of topics that need to be reviewed during sales seminars. Who are the seminar targeting? What kind of seminar do people want? Is it a form of discussion? Is it a simple form of lecture? Should I offer a seminar for free? Do I have to get paid? How can I get the venue? What is the importance of content that is informative and works as advertising? What should I do if someone interferes during the seminar? Should I be careful about holding a seminar that won't raise objections from anyone?

I was able to find answers to all of these questions by going to seminars regularly. I was fascinated by people standing in front of the public, especially politicians and entertainers, and studied what they said and how they were posted. Then I prepared my own sales seminar.

Sales seminars are a strong sales tool, and many companies use this tool. There are many factors that can help boost sales if the person who is providing a sales seminar is careful, and I want to cover some important things in this chapter.

First, it should be a seminar that is strictly informative. The presentation in the seminar should cover the topics fully and give complete information. The lecture alone should end by conveying full details. For example, Harulab conducts a seminar called "Write a Book in One Day." This lecture teaches you about the different ways you can write a book in one day and how to change your perspective on writing books. It also explains stereotypical reasons that have been holding you back from writing books. There's nothing that isn't explained in the seminar regarding writing a book in one day. If you go home with what you heard in the lecture and faithfully implement it on your own, you'll have the desired outcome.

There is no other secret know-how requiring further payment. However, it's natural to pay extra money to Harulab to continue receiving additional feedback, to utilize allied designers, or to work in a community, all of which are information and benefits that can't be provided in a one-time lecture.

Second, it should be a paid seminar.

As I mentioned above, a sales seminar should be a thorough, informative seminar. The seminar is meaningful in itself and should help participants. If a lecture is offered for free because it's intended to be a sales seminar, it will buy a sense of disillusionment.

This is because a free seminar won't give all of the information, and because people have the perception they'll receive more know-how when they pay for it. In particular, those who attend free lectures are often more price-conscious, and they're likely to complain about additional services when they're mentioned in a seminar.

Sales seminars focus on sales ultimately, but the attendees do not. There must be something to gain from the time itself. No one would be happy to pay more money to get more details. When I conduct a lecture, I ask people to ask me whatever questions they want to ask. I try to answer everything. In the meantime, I open everything I know to the attendees; the only limitation is the time.

Third, you shouldn't suddenly show your true colors during the seminar.

The most awkward method is to conduct a seminar early on and reveal products and prices by showing your true intention in the last chapter of the presentation. This will make people uncomfortable. This is because people who conduct seminars only care about the last page that introduces products in their heads.

When you open the last page, people's responses are cold, and you destroy the previous pages because you had to think about how to drive sales. If you have a product to sell through the seminar, you should work it in smoothly in the middle of the seminar.

"You mean I should have an ad in the middle?"

This way seems even more difficult. You have to tell an engaging story, not make a direct advertisement. When a product being sold is mentioned in the middle, it becomes excellent information and natural advertising.

As an example, if you were giving a lecture on building an automated sales process online, you could inform customers about how to make web pages easily, how to bring potential customers to the web page, how to create loyalty from potential customers, and how to communicate with customers who demonstrate loyalty.

You could then naturally bring up the subject of programs like the company's own automated email tools. In fact, you could show examples of results from using these tools. That naturally would raise questions about such email tools. At the end of the lecture, at the time of questions and answers, the attendees would naturally ask about the tools. Then, you could tell them about the product or program and tell the price.

Talking about a product because attendees asked a question gives a different impression than unilaterally promoting a product by putting it in the presentation. It will minimize the resistance. Don't ruin the impressive experience of your seminar with a clumsy sales presentation at the end.

When designing a sales seminar in detail, there are many things to consider, but I mentioned the points the presenter is most likely to miss.

11. The 100 x 100 x 100 method to operate sales automation.

As mentioned earlier, my first book is *I Work Only Four Hours a Week and Earn 10 Million Won a Week.* In this book, I explain that if you're buried in a way that you have repeated in the past, you can't enjoy real freedom in your life. If you think a thorough labor-based revenue generation is the only way, you can't create a situation like that book title. In that sense, I was told that if the words in my title were true, they would bring about the collapse of the labor market. The story inside of the book is not at all about ditching labor. But if you look at the title only, you'd naturally think that's what I'm saying. The main message of the book is this: "You can't wish to live in a different way in the future if you stick to your old way of living."

Living a hard-working life in the past doesn't change the future. I find this situation well reflected in the numerous stories of those who quit their jobs after working hard.

Even if you work harder and get promoted faster, what you'll see is your seniors and your bosses, whose lives don't look so happy either. They don't even look healthy as they are so busy.

Still, there's no guarantee that quitting your job will make you happier than they are. However, it's definitely possible to take a different path from the past. You can learn new ways that you didn't know in the past. Seeing that people change a lot just by being given such a choice, I actually am careful in recommending someone to quit their job. Nonetheless, in a real crisis, people know their limits and potential. I was also a similar case. After I lived a life of irregular work with no stable income, I achieved explosive personal growth. I was able to throw away my past self because I had the desire to survive.

There are common characteristics in some of the members of Butterfly Investment who are growing slowly but suddenly changed rapidly while reading documents, videos, and lectures produced by Butterfly Investment. They either quit their jobs or quit school. They put down what they thought was important in the past, focused more on their current self, and found their real potential. Of course, this was possible because senior entrepreneurs from Butterfly Investment who have gone through this path have given advice and led them.

It's been more than five years since I'm living a life free from work and free from the early morning commute.

I can go to the theaters and markets anytime I want during weekdays, and I can travel abroad with my family whenever I want. This is a life that can never be achieved just because it's aimed at making a lot of money. If Butterfly Investment had more employees and more physical stores, it would make more income, but there would be more restrictions on freedom. We see this in countless businesses around us.

To enjoy more freedom in daily life, the sales process should be automated, customer follow-ups should be automated, and there should be no irregular tasks that hold you back. Fixed costs should also be minimized. Naturally, such a system is not built automatically from the beginning.

Usually, business owners try to build such a system in the later stage, but it's not easy because they have to tear up their business model and build a new one from scratch.

Strong commitment and the desire to live such a free life are needed from the start. One more thing is to put away the obsession of such a life. This sounds like a conflict—not being obsessed with having such a system but having a strong attachment. This relates to what people call "the laws of attraction." Those who write their goal 100 times every day also advise this. You have to be attached, think of yourself constantly, and write your goals first if you wish to have this system.

However, you shouldn't be obsessed if it doesn't happen right away. Successful people don't obsess, because they believe it will happen eventually. If you don't separate the attachment and obsession, you could fall into great despair. Adherence and obsession should be completely separated. Obsession brings impatience, impatience leads to mood swings, and they lead to unnecessary energy waste. Obsession can never bring about the desired change in your life.

Impatience is a common trait of people who stick to the ways they've lived in the past. They're impatient because they believe that the 10 or 20 years they've experienced were meaningful enough and will be reflected in their future. It's not about changing their lives. This thinking reflects an arrogant mind.

If the past 10 or 20 years were meaningful enough and were satisfying, you shouldn't be unhappy, or want to change now. If you live a life that isn't satisfactory, you're showing that you have to live a life differently from the past. You should start right away when you decide to live differently. The past is not necessary. You need to build your own content again. From now on, you have to record the process of finding what you want to do. Or, if you already found what you want to do, you should study it and create new content starting today.

I founded Butterfly Investment with Choi in order to prevent businesses from going bankrupt, and future generations of their families from falling apart. The spirit of the zero-base startup is being refined and spread to the public. In the process, I've produced over 2,000 pages of business-idea documents. Separately, 200 newsletters have been created that intend to motivate entrepreneurs to start a zero-base startup. There are about 100 articles to inspire entrepreneurs. In addition, the story of business pirates is available to listen to in a series of over 100 podcasts, "The Pirates' Startup Story." There are more than 300 video clips in the YouTube channel "Zero-Base Startup" (ZERO).

I also published paper books and e-books on the internet. On top of that, if the cases of those who succeed with their zero-base startup and their content are added together, the majority of content related to zero-base startup is distributed by Butterfly Investment, not only in Korea but also in the world.

With 100 pieces of quality content in each modality—text, voice, and video—sales were generated automatically. And I even enjoyed creating that content. I can't help but have fans. Publishers keep contacting me, and I receive requests to appear on TV shows and as a guest lecturer.

Companies cofounded by Butterfly Investment are also slowly experiencing this as their content accumulates and is built diligently online. In particular, what I'm most proud of is that a growing number of people are realizing the first-contact experience from customers who respond to the accumulated content, without having to go around to make sales. Founders should be able to make content out of what they're doing. Usually, they don't think they have time to make content as they're too busy. Of course, there's no guarantee that the content you're making right now will bring you immediate revenue.

If you don't have the time to create online content, you may think that the business model needs to be modified. You must spend the rest of the time creating content while initially experiencing intense customer and sales meetings. I'm still doing the same and continue to give this mission to fellow entrepreneurs. This explains why it's difficult for workers and self-employed people who work hard all day to earn more revenue and freedom at the same time.

It's because there's no room and time to create their own online content in order to convey the worthy work they're doing. The longer they're buried at their job, the further they are from founding a business, the harder it is for them to make their own mark, and the further they are from being free.

Once again, there's no intention to devalue labor. Rather, this is more like how to raise the value of labor. If you want to start a business, make time to look at your labor values. Such observations are necessary to be recorded, and records can be refined as fine content.

When there are hundreds of such content stacked up, you'll realize the value of your work.

Be sure to remember this: A person with no patience can never create the content of 100 texts, 100 podcasts, or 100 video images. No matter how well you can write and handle computer technology, it doesn't produce tangible content like this. It's only possible for those who start from scratch with strong conviction and humility. I think this thought will definitely help you because it's insight from advising and producing results for thousands of would-be entrepreneurs.

12. Data analysis and A/B tests and sales

As the Fourth Industrial Revolution becomes an issue, it's often reported that the future of data analytics experts will be promising. That's why the training for Python—a programming language used in data analytics—is so popular these days. It's no exception for startups to make money to analyze vast amounts of data. Even if you start an online shopping mall, you should keep track of your potential customers' buying patterns, and manage products that sell well and products that don't sell well. We're able to customize ads for customers because we can analyze customer data.

Facebook and Google have big data about users who are logged on to their services and are conducting online activities. Based on this data, we can advertise according to a customer's age, location, online purchasing activity, and interests.

It's not just about advertising. You can also track the performance of the homepage and whether it's a good page for making sales. You can determine whether the posts on the homepage are capturing people's attention or if site visitors are leaving as soon as they see the ads. Free services such as Google Analytics allow us to analyze how much content on the website is optimized for sales. You can modify or remove content that analysis shows aren't efficient, and leave only the content that is efficient.

The content that creates a transition to sales can be different from the content that attracts traffic. However, without these analytical frames, it's easy to conclude that just getting a lot of traffic is good. Therefore, while there's a large influx of visitors to websites because of stimulating titles, there are also a lot of inefficient homepages with high rates of losing customers. If there is a lot of traffic, management costs will go up. However, if potential customers stay on the homepage less time due to lack of content management, and there are fewer page views, the product is not converted to actual sales. You'll continue to pour water into the sunken jar. Data analysis functions as a prevention to patching up the broken jar. Knowing what content is driving away potential customers will allow you to make changes to prevent these customers from being left out. Putting products in a shopping basket and offering coupons to customers who are worried about making payments are tasks that prevent loss of business. Data analysis shows how to prevent customers from leaving the market during the purchasing process.

Data analysis doesn't only reduce the number of customers deserting the homepage and help you create highly efficient content. Data analysis also enables efficient use of advertising costs. When a company spends $1,000 in advertising fees and reaches 10,000 potential customers, 10 percent of them could end up providing $10,000 in sales revenue for you. However, if you spend $500 for advertising and reach 5,000 customers who are expected to have a higher purchasing rate, 20 percent of them could provide $10,000 in sales revenue for you.

One example is the advertising cost of $1,000, but in fact, many companies spend $10,000 or $100,000, a month on advertising alone. The higher the advertising cost, the more important advertising efficiency becomes, and the difference in product purchase rate and customer conversion rate has a significant impact on sales and costs. That's why businesses utilize data analytics to try to find a group of customers with a high conversion rate. Companies are also making efforts to increase the conversion rate by creating customized advertisements for target customers.

As part of such attempts, there's also an A/B test. In brief, A/B tests show which type of advertisement will be opened up and which type of advertisement will allow more customer input or payment.

If you test three copies and focus on the most popular advertising copy, this will certainly improve efficiency. Most startups are using Facebook targeted ads or Google AdWords. This is because Facebook and Google offer targeted advertising services that are optimized for target marketing based on vast data from users. However, simply setting a target that would like a product and setting a high advertising fee doesn't produce results.

Even if I sell products that targeted women, there may be different advertisements that will generate a response from different age groups or jobs. At this time, it's important to further refine the target and create a copy of the ad that matches the target. Landing pages coming in from the advertisement should also be tailored to the segmented target.

For example, if you're selling women's cosmetics while doing Facebook ads, you have to create an ad catch and image that match each target with a detailed target in mind, such as working moms, housewives, and college students. The ad image created for workers using Facebook target ads is to be exposed only to workers, to housewives, and to college students respectively.

Only when this granular work is done will the customers' response to the ad increase. Depending on the situation of each customer, the words that cause the need for cosmetics, for example, are different. Increasing the inflow to homepages through advertising isn't the end of the capture process.

After inflow, there should still be landing pages that reflect the feelings and mood received from the advertisements. Once the ad has been clicked, the content should be linked to and configured on the landing page. If a college student has been targeted by an ad and brought in, the landing page should be created in a way that a college student can relate to.

It sounds like plenty of work. If you're going to run the advertisement once or twice only, you don't have to consider this. However, companies that pay tens of thousands of dollars per month must consider this.

If the only alternative is to simply spend more on advertising costs as a way to make more revenue, the business won't last long. Butterfly Investment and zero-base entrepreneurs are known for rarely spending money on advertising. Some even go around openly saying, "Don't market at a cost if the quality of the product isn't high." Entrepreneurs should avoid the temptation to pay for high advertising costs because they're under the illusion the result will be a high sales revenue.

I won't stop you if you have tons of money to spare. However, people who are starting their own business as a zero-base startup are in a different position. They're constantly producing quality content to pursue a viable marketing process as the content and marketing interact with each other organically.

Zero-base startup entrepreneurs must run ads at minimal cost and devise strategies that are several times more efficient than anything else. To that end, the aforementioned data analysis and A/B tests are necessary. There's a Butterfly Investment member who designs excellent Facebook marketing and gives lectures about these details, Choi Gyu-Moon. His book—*The Facebook Guide*—will help you get access to the content mentioned in this chapter.

The use of data isn't just for online businesses. For nearly a year, I gave a different lecture every week on starting a private business. At the beginning of the lecture, I talked to people who attended and listened to their questions and situations. The information regarding the questions was followed by a prepared lecture. Of course, the participants responded well, and there was a positive impact on their companies' sales. This is also a small case of data analysis. In order to live as a zero-base startup entrepreneur with minimal advertising costs, such data approaches are naturally implemented.

Looking at this book, I hope you will be reborn as an entrepreneur free from the pressure of advertising fees.

Epilogue

"Even if the company collapses, the life of the founder should not be ruined."

Those who fail to keep pace with their company's growth are always at risk. This is because the company stops growing when the owner thinks that their personal growth is the most important influence on company growth but the owner stops their personal growth. An entrepreneur who puts sales first can continue to grow. They can lead the company's initial growth. They can appoint talented people, overcome limitations with them, and grow the company again. When a company starts to grow under the power of huge outside capital, these opportunities fly away quickly.

According to a 2014 survey by the KAIST Center for Entrepreneurship, 7.2 percent of the top executives in Korea who closed their business have restarted their business. This means that if one hundred people start a business, only seven are going back after they fail. Among the latter group, 21 percent say they are going out of business again. This means that few people can meet the challenges of running a business again after they fail.

It's never easy to dream of restarting a business when people have more debt than they can afford, and then their family collapses. In addition, if the reason for failure to keep a business is due to the environment and funding, then restarting the business will inevitably lead to the same mistakes as before.

What grade are you in when you go to elementary school, at age six? Even though you're six years old, you're just a first grader. The same holds true for startups. No matter how many times you start a business, no matter how long you've been starting it, the company's crisis is accompanied by the founder's crisis if the founder doesn't learn.

A person who has lived a lifetime as a consumer must study and switch to a supplier's way of thinking while preparing to start a business. A supplier who's biased towards consumers is concerned not only about themselves, but also about their employees, customers, and family. The journey to a creative and provider-minded entrepreneur begins with a close approach to sales. This is because it's realistic to think about how to make a profit while trying to sell the products, and how to manage internal and external customers. An entrepreneur should be able to sell to a handful of customers first and develop a more sophisticated product and maintain a high level of customer satisfaction without selling products at a lower price.

An entrepreneur who knows how to sell the high-satisfaction products to certain customers, how to respond to them, what content to use, and what partners or employees to work with profits from the system from the start and from their own labor. I call this phase the entrepreneur level. You'll never get to this stage unless you grow up with salespreneurship. When capital is invested and you have an uncompromised expansion, you have to deal with unmanaged situations and have constant troubles.

Entrepreneurs need to put sales first and go through trial and error early on so that they can reflect on more things when the company expands. If a person suffers from a problem that becomes bigger, he or she can't concentrate on preventing the problem. Businesspeople who have grown on a scale based on salespreneurship know the insignificance of competition. An entrepreneur is someone who's in the stage of business building with the hope that the whole business group in which they belong will be successful.

The only person who can be a true entrepreneur is a person who can show that their entrepreneurship has grown up completely based on salespreneurship.

Businesspeople who don't leave the sales scene have good sense. They can solve in just one hour what others have worried about for more than a year.

Entrepreneurs at the sales scene are always keen to self-manage. They take health seriously, choose good food, and exercise regularly because they need to manage the impression they give when meeting internal or external customers.

Also, entrepreneurs at the sales sites learn constantly. They even learn from their students and staff. They increase insight by newly accessing and learning new markets or project groups that weren't previously known. The entrepreneur at the sales scene is modest. They experience the emergence of areas they couldn't thread with their own insight. Through the stories on the ground, with new approaches, they try to thread the parts they couldn't get through previously. I believe there is nothing you can't do, but you can be humble because you know it's possible only when you find a clue on the ground.

Through this phase, entrepreneurs rise to become great entrepreneurs. A great entrepreneur is a person who does things for humankind. They're concerned beyond merely developing their own market. I think that a great entrepreneur is someone who creates a new world, thinking about how to solve the problems of hunger and global warming, and how to pioneer the universe.

Entrepreneurs like Elon Musk and Jeff Bezos are now leading the way. They're pushing for businesses that others say are crazy. They remain steady in the face of controversy because they believe they're doing great things and must do what they do. Electric vehicles, space exploration, and hyperloop projects are things that go beyond the corporate spectrum. I hope that great entrepreneurs who affect positive changes in our global world continue to appear.

Some people continue to look at me with suspicion as I spread the spirit of salespreneurship. I've been told this is a crazy business and doesn't make any sense. But I had great business teachers. I'm a person who lives on a promise to learn and grow today even if I die tomorrow. I also dream of becoming a great entrepreneur.

So I've zealously looked for items and tried to learn every day. By encouraging other entrepreneurs to discover such projects and raising zero-base startup entrepreneurs optimized for sales, Butterfly Investment is spreading a new business culture and ecosystem to the world.

Even if a company and business collapse, the founder's life doesn't have to be ruined. I can assure you that there will be a world of salespreneurs in the future. Even if a company goes bankrupt, the salesperson should have no fear of restarting their business. I'm convinced that only a salesperson who follows items that make their heart beat hard, contemplates the world with love, and considers sales a game can grow into a great entrepreneur.

I'm carrying on my business with an ambition to continue to spread the sales program to the world beyond Korea. I'm sure some of you are inspired by this book and will decide to live as salespreneurs. I look forward to establishing our sales motto- "Sales Is First!" around the world, and to becoming a great entrepreneur. And I also look forward to you becoming great entrepreneurs and to meeting again.

If you like this book, please leave your honest review on Amazon.

These reviews really help me as an author to get my book in front of more people just like you. Thank you!

© 2018 Taesoon Shin. All rights reserved.

About the Author

Taesoon Shin is the founder of Butterfly Investment, contents creator, and also singer and dancer. He has discovered the link between start-ups and spirituality, and continues to spread this sprit through numerous writings and videos.

Moreover, Shin is doing coaching focusing on changes in unconsciousness allows entrepreneurs to find answers for themselves to have successful business.

Currently, Shin is running Butterfly Investment, focusing on Zero-base Startup business (Guiding businesss owners to start their business with no money, or no investment). Butterfly Investment in Korea, which for the fifth year is spreading the know-how on Zero-base Startup created a number of successful startup cases and coaching practices based on the Zero-base Startup.

His other books are "I work four hours a week and make 10 million won" and ""The Pirates' Startup Story" (only available in Korean):

Butterfly Investment - an amazing company that provides entrepreneurs with new mindset as well as eye-catching business models that are totally new to the world. Butterfly Investment is guiding business owners to avoid half-grown businesses from external investments and loans from the start and help them to start businesses without capital-Zero-base Startup.

It is selling $1,000 membership based online and has already made 6 figure earnings with online sales only. Butterfly Investment created 30 companies with no capital, Zero-base Startup. Moreover, Butterfly Investment is also making profits by incubating these startup companies now.

If you are interested about the author and Butterfly Investment, please contact to below:

Email:Jihyekim.825@gmail.com

Instagram: www.instagram.com/shintaesoon

Web page: http://butterflyinvest.com/

© 2018 Taesoon Shin. All rights reserved.

www.ingramcontent.com/pod-product-compliance
Lightning Source LLC
Chambersburg PA
CBHW071632220526
45469CB00002B/583